Art &

Three-Dimensional **Experience**

NORMAN MANNERS

Series Editor Margaret Morgan

Hodder & Stoughton

A MEMBER OF THE HODDER HEADLINE GROUP

British Library Cataloguing in Publication Data
Manners, Norman
Three Dimensional Experience. – (Art & Design for Learning Series)
I. Title II. Series
372.5044

ISBN 0 340 611138

First published 1995
Impression number 10 9 8 7 6 5 4 3 2 1
Year 1999 1998 1997 1996 1995

Typeset by Wearset, Boldon, Tyne and Wear.
Printed in Great Britain for Hodder & Stoughton Educational, a division of Hodder Headline Plc, 338 Euston Road, London NW1 3BH by Scotprint Ltd, Edinburgh.

Contents

Series preface: Art and design for learning

Art and design for learning is a series of books which aims to provide a number of individuals involved in teaching with a platform from which to write about working with children and the thinking which lies behind their work.

The series authors are all experienced teachers and educationalists. They have had the privilege of visiting and working in schools, or of working with groups of teachers who have generously given permission for their children's work, and some of their own thoughts, to be included.

In the present climate of intense curriculum development created by the introduction of the National Curriculum for England and Wales, there is a great fear amongst some teachers that room for individuality and inventiveness is in danger of being lost. If this were to be the case, it would of course be disastrous, but it need not happen.

Research historians and cooks experimenting with fifteenth- and seventeenth-century bread and cake recipes encountered failure until they realised that the key ingredient was never listed. This was because all the practitioners knew it to be such a basic necessity that everyone concerned would already know about it. The unlisted ingredient was yeast.

The same principle could be applied to many of our curriculum documents. The yeast in art and design education must surely be the life, energy and individuality of the child and the teacher, working creatively with the ingredient of experience and the means. Any defined curriculum agreed upon by others and presented to an establishment, an authority, county or state is inclined to appear restrictive at first glance, especially if we personally have not been responsible for drafting it. What we are able to do with it will depend on whether we see it as a platform to work from, or a cage to be imprisoned in.

It is therefore very important to coolly appraise the nature and content of the work we are undertaking with the children in our schools and to think carefully about our personal philosophy and values. We need to identify areas of any imposed curriculum that we are in fact already covering and then consider those which call for development or may need to be introduced. It is only when we really understand the common denominator which lies behind these areas of experience that we can assimilate them into a holistic and coherent developmental pattern on which to base our strategies for practice.

In simple terms, any sound curriculum pertaining to art, craft and design must surely require a broad, balanced, developmental programme which has coherence and respects the experience, strengths and weaknesses of individual children, thereby enabling them to think, respond and act for themselves. Perhaps the real evaluation of a good teacher is to see whether children can proceed with their learning independently when he/she is no longer responsible for them.

The curriculum should make it possible to introduce children to the wonders and realities of the world in which we all live and should include art, craft and design forms from our own and other cultures and times. These can prove to be an enriching experience and can broaden the children's expectation of the nature of human response together with some experience of different ways of making art and design forms.

The curriculum should enable children to see the potential, and master the practice, of any relevant technologies, from the handling of simple hand tools to the world of information technology. It should enable them to work confidently in group and class situations as well as individually: thinking, making, appraising and modifying the work they are undertaking, negotiating skilfully with one another and discussing or talking about what they are doing, or have done. All of these aspects of education can be seen in the context of the National Curriculum which has, in the main, been based on some of the best practices and experience of work in recent years.

Intimations of the yeast component are clearly apparent in these selected extracts from *Attainment Targets and Programmes of Study for Key Stages 1 and 2.* (It is also very interesting to note the clear differences in requirements between the two stages; at seven and at eleven years of age. Stage 2 assimilates and develops Stage 1 requirements, building on them developmentally with specific additions.) At Key Stage 1 (seven years) the operative words are:

> investigating, making, observing, remembering, imagining, recording, exploring, responding, collecting, selecting, sorting, recreating, recognising, identifying, *beginning* to make connections . . . [my italics].

There is a very strong emphasis throughout on *direct experience, looking at* and *talking about*. At Key Stage 2 (eleven years) the following expectations are added:

> communicating ideas and feelings, developing ideas, experimenting [there is a subtle difference between exploration and conscious experimentation], applying knowledge, planning and making, choosing appropriate materials, adapting and modifying, comparing, looking for purposes, discussing . . .

What could be clearer in suggesting a lively educational experience? I believe that individuality and inventiveness are firmly based on having the right attitudes and they usually thrive best in the context of vehicles such as interest, happenings and the building up of enthusiasm and powerful motivation. The overall structure, balance and developmental nature of any sound curriculum model can allow content to flourish in lively interaction between children, teachers and the world of learning experiences.

If we persist in hardening the content of the National Curriculum in such a way that we are not able to manoeuvre or respond to the living moment, then we have ourselves forged the links of the chain which binds us.

The books in this series do not aim to be comprehensive statements about particular areas of art, craft and design experience, but they are vigorous attempts to communicate something of the personal, convinced practice of a number of enthusiastic professionals. We hope that they will also offer enough information and guidance for others to use some of the approaches as springboards for their own exploration and experience in the classroom.

Margaret Morgan
Series Editor

Preface

It is strange that three-dimensional art in schools is seldom seen to be of the same importance as two-dimensional creative and expressive work (it has been noted by Her Majesty's Inspectorate in surveys and reports). We live in a three-dimensional environment surrounded by three-dimensional things, both living and inanimate. We ourselves are three-dimensional beings with sensory equipment – eyes, hands, feet, skin, brain – which receives information about our world in the form of space, form, light and shadow, texture and colour. Perhaps our attitude towards three-dimensional work reflects our own education and the educational values which were implicitly and explicitly laid upon us. Where does the idea come from that 'real education' is somehow restricted to two-dimensional academic paperwork (together with the computer in present times), and abstract thought? There is a salutary true story of a headteacher showing a group of dignitaries around the school, and who, on coming to an incredibly mature piece of sculpture, explained that this was by one of the 'remedial children'!

Children who work in three dimensions in their early years can build up practical knowledge and understanding of the potential of materials, the development and sequencing of ideas as the work is changed and refined, and the nature of substances, weight, form and space to name but a few examples. The experience of manipulating, building and feeling, which so often generates creative activity, is of great importance from the pre-school years right through the primary years. There is no other experience which can replace it. The discipline of materials is one of the most basic lessons for us all to learn and unless we assimilate it, and are able to understand any material which is new to us, we are missing a very important ingredient in our functioning, and later our designing potential.

The National Curriculum has many references to the whole area of three-dimensional experience. These include, at Key Stage 1:

> selecting from a range of items [the children] have collected and using them as a basis for their work . . . collecting and sorting images, objects and source material

> . . . working practically and imaginatively with a wide variety of materials and methods exploring the elements of art . . . exploring a range of materials, tools and techniques . . . exploring and recreating pattern and texture in natural and made forms . . . exploring the use of shape, form and space in making images and artefacts . . . making three-dimensional work for a variety of purposes.

and at Key Stage 2:

> developing an idea or theme for their work, drawing on visual and other sources, and discussing their methods . . . experimenting with ideas suggested by different source materials and explaining how they have used them to develop their work . . . experimenting with, and applying their knowledge of the elements of art, choosing appropriate media . . . applying their knowledge and experience of different materials, tools and techniques, using them experimentally and expressively . . . experimenting with pattern and texture in designing and making images and artefacts . . . experimenting with ways of representing shape, form and space . . . planning and making three-dimensional structures using various materials and for a variety of purposes.

Norman Manners was until recently Senior Art Adviser in Norfolk, and continues to work with teachers and children. He is deeply committed to art and design education, and is well able to see it in the wider context of primary years learning. His enthusiasm, and that of the teachers and children, is apparent in the contents of this book, and he makes a strong case for children to be extended and their understanding deepened by means of a balance between two- and three-dimensional work.

One of the most exciting things about three-dimensional work is the way in which children respond to it. Watching children between the ages of five and seven years playing in a stream and setting about the self-appointed task of building a bridge from materials they found in the vicinity left no doubts in my mind of the potential for practical learning encapsulated in the task in hand. There were a number of lengths of metal and pieces of wood, but none were anywhere near the length necessary to span the water. Much discussion and trial and error led to the building of stone islands which became the piers on which to place the rigid materials. The result was much satisfaction in a bridge which was high enough to clear the water and stable enough for children, and even for adults to walk across.

I saw another example of a more decorative but equally self-rewarding nature when two children were playing in the fallen blossom of cherry trees in full bloom. They used the material to hand to make sculptural relief and patterns with complete concentration and involvement. They were building up a series of conical reliefs and clearing shapes and lines from the very green grass between. Sometimes they arranged the blossom petal by petal, and at other times scooped up great double handfuls. Finally they started playing with the materials, running them between their fingers and throwing them into the air, laughing as they floated down all over themselves and their 'sculpture'. At length they moved on through the park, leaving their work to be distributed by the wind. They had clearly enjoyed the whole experience enormously, and I personally cannot doubt the value of exploration, experimentation, learning about materials, making practical and aesthetic choices, and looking at what had been achieved.

Margaret Morgan
Series Editor

Acknowledgments

I would like to thank the many children and colleagues with whom it has been a privilege to work. Many of their ideas and attitudes have contributed to the development of this book.

I am particularly grateful for the warm welcome and cooperation I received during my visits to the following schools to take photographs:

Astley Primary School, Melton Constable
Breydon V.C. Middle School, Great Yarmouth
Hockham Primary School, Great Hockham
Northfields First School and Assessment Unit, Norwich
Reffley Primary School, Kings Lynn
Sandringham and West Newton C.E., V.A., Primary School
South Harford Middle School, Norwich
St. Mary's V.C. Middle School, Long Stratton

I am grateful to Jan Marshall and the Contact Gallery in Norwich for their help with the section on environments.

Margaret Morgan was generous in giving her time, experience and encouragement during the evolution of the text. There are many individuals who have contributed to this book in various ways and I apologise that it is not possible to name them all.

1 Learning through three-dimensional art and design

INTRODUCTION

Like many other teachers I believe that capturing the interest of children, involving them actively in their own work and building confidence and a feeling of self-worth provides the best basis for a good education. I also believe that working in three dimensions can offer wonderful opportunities for this involvement and development. Understanding the potential of three-dimensional work can help teachers to provide the best kind of experiential learning, which need not be confined to the art curriculum.

If we consider how we can incorporate three-dimensional work in our own teaching we can discover many areas of interest and potential, yet if we look at the curriculum it often seems that we are missing opportunities. Three-dimensional work is often seen as the poor relation of the two-dimensional approach, in spite of the fact that it is far more directly related to our experience. We are three-dimensional beings in a three-dimensional world, surrounded by forms existing in space, shown to us by light and shadow, involving surfaces of different textural qualities.

There sometimes appears to be an innate fear amongst teachers considering three-dimensional work as to their ability to cope. The practical problems of dealing with quantities of bulky materials, as well as a lack of technical knowhow intimidate many teachers. Others worry about being able to judge work appropriately and these worries override our understanding of the value of three-dimensional experiences to children. More insidious is the attitude that three-dimensional work is less important or significant than two-dimensional work, or that children must be able to plan in two dimensions before they can undertake three-dimensional challenges. A narrow interpretation of design and the design process can exacerbate this misunderstanding further and it is useful for all of us to challenge these attitudes. Children and adults naturally learn through touch as well as vision, whether in the context of art or everyday life and we all handle solid forms of all kinds. Experience of texture, mass and form in natural items such as fruit, pebbles, shells, timber, water, sand, and in made objects like pottery, tools, containers, furniture, and on a larger scale, buildings and vehicles, is part of our growing understanding of the way the world works.

Children learn in many ways, by investigation and exploration, by personal response and imagination, through experiences and by being encouraged to make use of what they know. Practical skills can be developed by many means, including personal challenge, demonstration, following instructions in the use of tools and equipment safely and, of course, practice. Teaching situations require combinations of these, depending on what is to be learned and the ability and individuality of the child. Each route can involve three-dimensional activities, either as the direct objective for the work or as the way to fulfilling and enhancing the topic or theme.

As a teacher I have found that most children respond enthusiastically to working in three dimensions. They naturally enjoy exploration and experimentation with materials and the tangible evidence of their own responses and ideas. The outcomes, being solids in space, have their own existence, a sense of being real, as well as, in some cases, representing things from the children's experience of the world. These qualities often give children a more intense feeling of the significance of their work and a greater sense of ownership and pride.

We in turn need to learn to appreciate the child's ability at each stage, and to find ways of helping to develop understanding and skills. Through this approach we can ensure that lessons are appropriate and our actions as teachers provide effective education.

All children need experience of materials in order to understand them, and it is a delight to watch even very young children 'playing' or rather 'exploring' sand, clay, dough, water, threads, fibres, wood and other natural materials, as well as items made of plastic, metal or timber. Appropriate challenges can be used to lead children to respond personally to the experience of materials, tools and equipment. Our teaching should enable children to develop steadily, which means using appropriate stimulation by surrounding them with interesting forms and textures and encouraging their awareness of them, including works by artists and designers.

There are, of course, overlaps and parallels between two- and three-dimensional work and one can lead to the other, whichever experience comes first. Perhaps the most important issue to consider is the need for real practical experience with materials, their potentials and limitations, prior to 'designing' or making initial drawings of possible solutions. It is only possible to design effectively when you 'know' a material. Relationships between forms and spaces, and matters of structure and surface quality can be examined in three dimensions – using a suitable material – whether the final work is to be in two or in three dimensions. This holds good for adults as well as children and many artists and designers make models or maquettes prior to producing their finished work. Wax figures by Rembrandt, clay or plaster sketches by Edgar Degas or Henry Moore, car body forms in clay by designers are a few of the many examples which could be chosen.

Working in three dimensions can be based on firsthand experience, for example, reconstructing the form of an animal or building that we have seen, or it can be more abstract, perhaps exploring the behaviour of a material. It can help us to explore our relationship with our surroundings, and the people and animals in them, and with the many cultures with which we have contact. We may experience a sense of curiosity, wonder and awe during this exploration. This can be the start of the growth of our spiritual feelings and our understanding of our place in the world.

WORDS AND MEANINGS

Words are keys to our understanding and it is very important to consider how we use them with our children and how we encourage them to communicate and express their ideas to us. Within the context of this book I think it would be useful for me to say something of the particular meanings of some of the words I shall be using.

The elements of art

The National Curriculum lists 'Elements of art' as:

> line, tone, pattern and texture,
> colour, shape, form and space.

Each of these has a part to play in three-dimensional work.

Line

Line is often understood as a continuous mark on a flat surface, but can equally be a movement through space in three dimensions, for example, a drawing with a piece of wire to represent the rhythm and structure of branches and twigs.

Tone

Tone involves the lightness or darkness of surfaces, which can be an important aesthetic or design consideration. Light tones reveal the subtlety of a surface, contrasts add clarity and sparkle.

Pattern

Pattern is linked to the order which exists in practically everything in our lives. It involves repetition of similar or related units, and enables us to predict and understand language, number, environment and society. Art and design is often concerned with identifying patterns, but also with breaking from the predictable to new ground, in order to explore fresh ideas and find variety.

Colour

Colours of materials and the finishing layers of paint or glaze which we can apply provide us with a rich language with which to represent, express or fulfil our enjoyment of colour.

Shape

Shape – a two-dimensional quality – is frequently a part of three-dimensional work, whether in the form of decoration or subdivision on a surface, or the overall silhouette shape of a sculpture or a pot seen against the light.

Three-dimensional work makes particular use of form, space and texture; to this list of elements I have added structure. Everything around us includes these elements. In the examples illustrated one element is dominant.

Form

Form has many meanings, but in the context of three-dimensional work it describes solid shapes in space, and their surface convexities, concavities, edges and planes (see figures 1a and b). Form may give an indication of mass and weight or internal structure, but may conceal an unpredictable interior. Is an egg shape made of the same material throughout, or is it a shell containing a yolk? Is the inside of a capsicum solid, like an apple? Children love to find out. They enjoy stroking surfaces – exploring the form – of a pet or a piece of bark (figures 1c and d). Manipulating materials such as clay allows them to produce all kinds of forms and to change them easily in response to their imagination or their desire for accurate representation. (See figures C2, C3, C4, C5, C6 and C7 on page 114 of the colour section.)

Figure 1a

Figure 1b

Figure 1c

Figure 1d

Figures 1a–1d are examples of form

Figure 2a

Figure 2b

Figure 2c

Figure 2d

Figures 2a–2d are examples of space

Space

Working in three dimensions involves creating objects in a space. Size, scale, distance, relative position and movement are all part of the use of space. As every tangible thing in the world occupies space, its existence can be seen in terms of the space around it. Conversely, we see space in terms of the objects within it, or the things which contain the space.

Open space in gardens and in the countryside can allow our minds the freedom to escape from the mundane (see figure 2a). So too can buildings, even if they are essentially designed as spaces for us to use and inhabit.

Children are more aware of objects than their place in space to begin with, but they are very interested in holes within forms and enjoy exploring them (see figures 2b, c and d). They are fascinated by caves, tunnels, mouths, knot holes and so on. They also enjoy grouping objects, putting things into containers, stacking, scattering and using objects to define boundaries of space. (See figures C8, C9, C10, C11, C12 and C13 on page 115 of the colour section.)

Texture

Rough or smooth, hard or soft, plain or irregular, the warmth of wool or the cold of marble, surfaces have many parts to play in our lives. Smooth for cleaning or for aerodynamic efficiency, rough to give grip, textures can intrigue the eye or hand. Our aesthetic sensibility responds readily to these qualities and ordinary surfaces can be given visual interest by their texture. Texture is, nevertheless, a tactile thing. In some cases it is about how we imagine it would feel, even though we may not be able to touch the surface itself. Texture is about pattern on a surface (see figures 3a, b, c and d), which often results from the properties of the material which is used, so handling materials is usually a vital part of experiencing these surface qualities.

Figures 3a–3d are examples of texture

Figure 3a

Figure 3b

Figure 3c

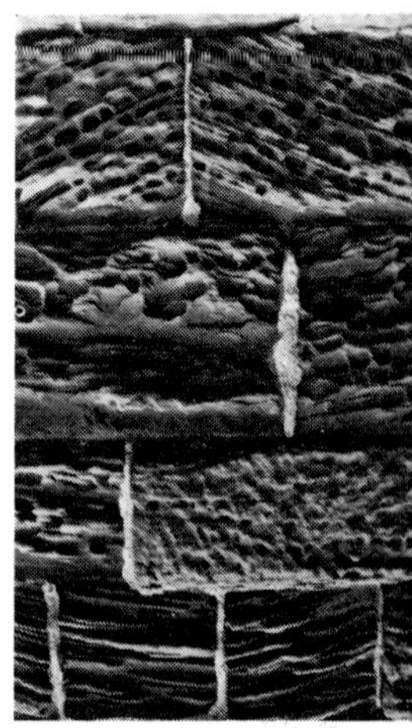

Figure 3d

Children are intrigued by the way things feel and need no encouragement to explore texture – by touching or stroking – or create their own textures in clay. 'Feely' boxes, containing objects of different textures which cannot be seen, making rubbings, and searching for and inventing words to describe textures, are always popular activities. (See figures C14, C15, C16, C17, C18 and C19 on page 116 of the colour section.)

Structure

Any three-dimensional object has to maintain its shape in some way. This may be achieved by the structure of the material itself, such as fibres in a tree or fabric, or the particles in clay, or by an integral skeleton (figure 4a). Other things stand through the use of struts or props which compress or extend (figures 4b, c, d and e). Structure can involve invisible means, such as electro-magnetic forces and those to be found in molecules at one extreme and the universe at the other. What is it that keeps things in position and so retains their spatial relationship to or contact with other things?

Figure 4a

Figure 4b

At an early age, children make piles of blocks or boxes (and then knock them down!). Later they readily involve themselves with constructional activities of a more complex nature. (See figures C20, C21, C22, C23, C24 and C25 on page 117 of the colour section.)

Figure 4c

Figure 4d

Figure 4e

Figures 4a–4e are examples of structure

There are other key words and phrases which we use in three dimensional work:

Light and shadow

In order to see anything we need light. The kind of light, its colour, intensity and spread can affect the appearance of objects and space. Concavities and convexities are revealed or concealed by the direction of the light. Areas of light and shade work together to reveal the form. Surfaces can be made to look richly textured or flat according to the angle of the light source. Backlighting – placing a model against a window, for example – can make us aware of the profile rather than the three-dimensional form.

Children are fascinated by light and enjoy playing with a light source shone on models or objects so that shadows are created, or particular parts are highlighted.

Work in the round

Objects which allow us access from every side can be described as being 'in the round'. We may see things from one viewpoint initially, but through raising, lowering or turning the object or using the spaces around it we can explore every facet.

Relief

There are many architectural situations where decoration or communication of stories, ideas or themes is achieved by building out from, or carving into a surface. This can be in low relief where there are very slight differences in depth between the highest and lowest parts, perhaps achieved through texture, inscribing or slight modelling of the surface. High relief can incorporate fully three-dimensional forms attached to or growing out from a background.

Touch

Three-dimensional work is about tactile sensitivity. Children need to understand different materials and their properties – the way they feel, their hardness, plasticity or elasticity – so that they can assess their suitability for different tasks. Tactile sensitivity is also about appreciation of materials' qualities – enjoyment through touch. For those with visual impairment, touch can be a vital means of learning and pleasure, a means of finding out about all manner of objects and materials, forms and structures and a way into learning about how things work.

Symbolism

Symbols are the representations which are made of some object or idea which are generally accepted as typifying its inherent qualities, usually in a simplified form.

The symbols that young children commonly use in their drawn images are well known and easily identified. A person is represented by a circle with attached sticks for arms and legs and very often no apparent body. A rectangle with a small square in each corner is a symbol for a house, bungalow or a block of flats with windows. These provide an effective means for a young child to communicate. In three-dimensional work, a similar use of symbols can be found, though the variety of materials may make them less easy to identify as being common. Heads modelled in clay may have spheres or indentations to represent each of the features. A building's windows will be arranged in a similar way to those on its drawn symbol. I have noticed that the challenge of making models in three dimensions can bring about a greater understanding of the shape or form of the original, which has then resulted in greater sophistication in drawn images.

Analysis

This links closely with the way children approach image-making. Objects are often conceived as an assemblage of pieces: a face is a number of separate features, an animal is a set of components. Analysis also means selecting the elements which are relevant for a particular purpose, and quite often changing the scale in relation to other parts. It involves teasing out and identifying specific qualities, such as the different textures, linear structures or underlying patterns in objects or situations. It is a way of learning on which we can capitalise when teaching, thereby helping our children to understand, from their observations of reality, the underlying principles of the way things are.

Imagination

Imagination involves seeing images in the mind which may come from our experience of reality or from fantasy. Imagination can be the repository for images from the past, or used as a way of visualising what could be. It enables us to bring together objects and experiences from diverse sources and place them into one situation in our minds. Imagination can help us to explore the potential of materials and structures and consider functional matters. It leads us to ask, and answer, such questions as:

What would that surface feel like if I could touch it?

How can we make a structure secure and visually attractive?

What would it be like to live in a different time or environment?

How many alternative forms could be used to fulfil this design task?

What is inside a machine, which we cannot see, but from our previous knowledge probably makes the thing work?

Where are the internal components and how does our body work?

What is the relationship between the angles, edges or surfaces in a geometric form?

What would happen if a particular thing was moved into a different position or context? (furniture in a room, tree in a garden, or building in a landscape)

What will happen to the plant as it grows bigger? How much space will it need?

Children's imagination needs constant feeding, restoring and exercising as part of education, and three-dimensional activities provide vital experiences to support this.

Images in our minds may be in two or three dimensions. For example, sculptors, architects, designers, engineers and surgeons all need the ability to visualise things both as a whole and in detail. They need to build a mental picture of the relationships between parts, the structural forces and the nature of the materials they are dealing with. These spatial aspects of imagination need specific experience and training, which begin with the very simple and direct actions of young children handling a variety of forms, textures and materials, steadily building up a vocabulary of experiences, knowledge and ideas. The act of using materials to create tangible forms in space as reconstructions of things seen can implant more profound images and understanding in the mind.

Fantasy

We sometimes confuse fantasy with imagination and there is, of course, some overlap. However, the essential feature of fantasy is its distance from reality – many fantasies are extravagant, and even impossible. Despite this, fantasy has real value, particularly in the way that it helps us to develop greater understanding about aspects of our existence. This is achieved by creating a world in our minds parallel to reality, which helps us to find solutions to problems. By freeing the mind from reality it gives access to new ideas and approaches. Fantasy is often to do with relationships and our emotional life and it can provide an escape from unacceptable situations. Three-dimensional models provide a means of creating fantasy situations and happenings, which have their own convincing reality. Children work out all manner of issues in this way as an essential part of learning and growing.

Create and creativity
This can be seen as taking the necessary action to make an object or an event, or even simply producing a thought, but in art and design it should be a more significant activity. The act of being creative involves bringing together experience, knowledge, imagination, and sometimes fantasy, in order to generate a personal response, expression of feelings, representation or design proposal. Fulfilling this amalgamation of thinking processes is usually achieved through the mental challenge of tasks combined with the use of practical knowledge and skills.

These are the kinds of words that children need in order to talk about their work, especially as part of the discussion before making modifications to their task in hand and for self-assessment. A vocabulary which describes concepts understood by children can be built up steadily through the application of words to experience of work by peers and adults.

Words such as 'imagination' and 'creativity' take complete books to define and to show their educational value. As teachers we need to develop our awareness of the importance to children of these faculties, particularly in their potential as a means of learning. We must ensure that the children have opportunity to experience the full meaning and power of these ways of thinking. This has many implications for our planning of the curriculum, the nature of specific lessons and our teaching approach.

'Creative' lessons can be the result of creative preparation, but do they always allow the children to think creatively?

2 Three-dimensional work across the curriculum

A VEHICLE FOR LEARNING

Art and design, including three-dimensional work, have their own special functions in our lives and in education. They are a means of communicating responses, ideas, opinions, emotions, a reflection of our culture and an opening to creative thinking and action. Inevitably, therefore, they touch other areas of activity or curriculum subjects. Taken a step further, art and design, and three-dimensional work in particular, can be used as a vehicle for learning across the curriculum.

Art and design must always be experienced and evaluated first and foremost in its own right if it is also to have validity in the context of cross-curricular work. In no way am I suggesting that the potential of art and design education can be fulfilled if it is used merely as a means of delivering the other disciplines, any more than we might consider there to be no need for language education because we happen to speak and write in every part of the curriculum. Real cross-curricular involvement must mean the use of the best strengths that each discipline has to offer.

There is an easily recognised richness in work which has a real aesthetic quality of line, form, colour or structure. This is seldom to be attained by simplistic challenges to 'draw it', or 'model it', tacked on to another subject challenge. A heightening of awareness of visual or tactile characteristics and qualities needs to be built into the experience. Sculpture and modelling especially need very careful consideration both in terms of their aesthetic quality and their real educational content.

How much, for example, do children learn about a timber-framed house and its construction by painting an upturned shoe box? Would it not be better to build a collage relief, or construct a section of the building, using wood to discover the real structure? Models of this kind should be an aid to understanding and consideration of design from the early years.

Three-dimensional models can be used to explore and represent themes either from one area of the curriculum, or embracing a group of subjects.

A large proportion of learning involves images in two or three dimensions. Photographs, illustrations, diagrams, actual objects – natural and made – all provide us with information about environment, society, culture and technology. The visual language also provides us with a means of reconstructing, and thereby testing, our understanding in any of these areas.

The organisation of primary schools gives us opportunities to work in a cross-curricular way, avoiding arbitrarily imposed boundaries, but still covering the requirements of individual subject areas. This can enable subjects to complement each other, enrich learning and help children learn in a way which relates more closely to the way the world operates. Analysis of the aims of each subject as stated in the National Curriculum reveals that there are huge areas of shared concern on which to base the planning of cross-curricular work, much more than is suggested in the brief cross-curriculum section in each Order.

National Curriculum requirements see cross-curricular links largely in terms of common areas of content, but I prefer to look at the practicalities of teaching as a whole, where it becomes clear that many of the processes of education are similar, or complementary, and often more vital than specific content. In a world which is increasingly dependent on visual means of communicating, children need the ability to 'read' visual images. Information and reference material may be in the form of photographs, moving images, drawings, diagrams or actual objects, each of which may require analysis, selective or discriminative decisions, leading to deductions and the assimilation of relevant information. The reading of images must not be taken for granted. It should be included as part of our teaching. We also need to ensure that children can produce forms and images that reconstruct experiences and convey their own thinking, responses and ideas, as well as enabling the teacher to monitor what has been assimilated. These abilities need regular use and practice.

The tangible nature of three-dimensional objects and the making of solid things can be particularly convincing to children. Touching, handling, walking round to view from all sides provides a much richer experience than a two-dimensional image, whether measured in terms of conveying information or the satisfaction that comes from creating things of substance (see figure 5).

Figure 5 Creatures in their environment, in modelled clay (age 8)

Every subject in the curriculum calls for thinking in inventive and creative ways at some stage, for example in formulating a hypothesis prior to testing, or when approaching a new and unfamiliar concept. The materials which are used in three-dimensional artwork allow rapid and free exploration of ideas and complex detail as well as being easy to refine or modify. This flexibility can itself stimulate creativity and inventiveness.

Three-dimensional models which describe situations and relationships can be used to explore the moral and ethical questions which are a feature of environmental and social studies. A model can make things seem more real than words alone.

INTERDEPENDENT ACTIVITIES

English

Art and design work provides an excellent means of stimulating children to use language in analytic, descriptive, deductive and expressive ways. I find that tangible items, either the children's own work or that of others, can be a helpful spur to producing language.

Description, analysis and surmising is so much easier for children with items which can be held and touched and can lead to fruitful conversation and writing as well as vocabulary extension. Children with learning difficulties often find that they can talk more readily about what exists in front of them, rather than about abstract issues. Questions such as 'what is it?', 'what is it made of?', 'how was it made?', 'when?' and 'why?' can be more productive and precise when the item is in front of the children. I have witnessed some wonderful, confident talks by children describing how they made their model.

A class of ten year olds were asked to bring in nouns and adjectives which occurred to them between home and school, and these were assembled on the blackboard:

> broken tree rubbish iron gates posters old car
> street signs holes in the road decaying tree stump
> curly fungi tumbledown fence broken window
> colourful flowers

and so on.

The children wrote a descriptive passage around one or more of the words, imagining a complete context and an event that could happen there. They planned and carried out a model to illustrate their idea using any available materials they wished, such as card, scrap materials and clay. Some chose to work in relief as they had worked in that way before, others worked in the round. They were encouraged to go back to their writing from time to time and to adjust their written ideas and descriptions as a result of working out their three-dimensional images.

There are many opportunities for exciting three-dimensional interpretations of literature, including poetry and drama. Children can produce a model of a context for a story or drama, or create a Jabberwocky, treasure island, or secret garden.

The visit of an artist, poet, theatrical or musical group from any culture can be the start of extensive and lively work in many areas. On a number of occasions I have seen a whole school absorbed in activities for several days as a result of such a visit. The activities did not adhere strictly to the set curriculum, but were very productive in terms of language extension, and the children learned a whole range of new skills through their intense and interested application. The strength of this approach is the natural way that children move freely and with purpose from one mode of working to another, crossing subject boundaries in pursuit of the challenge.

Mathematics

I am sure that early mathematical concepts are best taught in a three-dimensional way, using objects in space, grouping, adding, dividing, classifying, putting them into containers and so on. This applies to all children but is especially useful for those who have problems with mathematics. Seeing real life applications can give children a basic understanding and confidence that allows them to extend into areas requiring more abstract mental gymnastics. Just as art is concerned with developing a sense of visual pattern, so mathematics has to apply this sense to the handling of numbers.

The National Curriculum specifies that children should construct, describe and measure three-dimensional models, explore symmetry, and assess relative size and mass (see figures C26 and C27 on page 118 of the colour section). Materials such as clay, card and wire give easy means of investigating these themes and can develop from, or lead to, written or figurative work.

Geography

Much geography is concerned with investigating the physical environment, whether we are looking at local buildings or working out how buildings are made and used in other places (see figures C28 and C29 on page 119 of the colour section). Hills and valleys, slopes, rivers, roads, settlements, all make more sense when seen in reality or as a three-dimensional model, and more still when children (at an appropriate stage of development) are involved in the production of the model on which they can place grids and analyse contours.

A clay slab draped over a suitable support can provide children with an immediate hill or island with geographical features such as rivers, cliffs, caves, cols and tors, onto which buildings, hedges, trees and roads can be built (see figures 6a and b). For larger scale work, papier-mâché on wire mesh may be more suitable (see figure C30 on page 119 of the colour section).

The nature of soil, rock and water and the way they change was explored by a group of children who produced a series of clay models

Figure 6a Island made from a clay slab (age 7)

Figure 6b Island made from a modelled and textured clay slab (age 9)

which showed cross-sections of the sea shore at different points along a coastline (see figure 7). The models illustrated the relationship between the sea, beach, sand, cliffs and sand dunes, and enabled the children to study erosion factors.

The National Curriculum also requires children to have a sense of place by understanding their own locality, and from this to be able to imagine other locations. The route to school could be described by the use of the sand tray. The village or town's main street could be examined through the use of clay or card facades as a result of measuring, drawing and writing to assemble information. Or we may want to use fully three-dimensional models, of card or clay, to work out the arrangement and growth of the settlement, communication network or the construction of a particular building.

There are also rich educational possibilities in collecting artefacts and reproductions from different parts of the world just as it is important to build up well illustrated books for the school library.

History

Children find it far easier to understand history (and other cultures) when they have direct contact with artefacts from the period or culture they are learning about. Domestic utensils, clothing, jewelry and furniture give us clues about family and social life. Public buildings, street and road layouts, boats and other samples of industrial archeology tell us about a community. Religious, cultural, military and political events are depicted on pottery, relief panels and by sculptures. Through reconstruction or model-making, children

Figure 7 Beach and cliff, a clay model made from observation (age 11)

Figure 8 Portico, made in card, pasted paper and paint (age 10)

can gain insights into the significance of historical evidence as well as the specific events or use of objects (see figures 8 and 9).

A visit to the Museum of Mankind to see the display of the Mexican Festival of the Day of Death produced sheets of notes and drawings. Back at school the children selected their own theme individually or in small groups and produced models of figures, masks and the 'Tree of Death' (see figure 10, and figure C31 on page 120 of the colour section), mostly with wire and papier-mâché, which were painted and varnished. I have no doubt that the combination of talking and making developed greater depths of understanding than the visit alone.

Sculptures in the form of busts and statues can provide information about the life and times of other people, and carved friezes or doors and relief panels can record domestic, community, military or religious events from the past (see figure C32 on page 120 of the colour section).

Figure 9 Oil lamps made from fired and painted pinch pots (age 9)

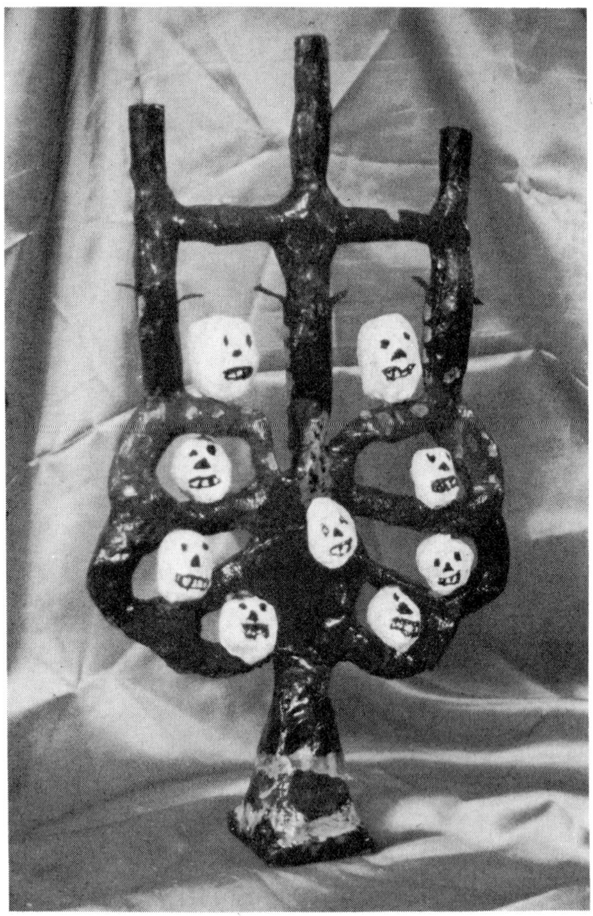

Figure 10 Tree of the Day of Death, made with wire, papier-mâché and paint (age 10)

Science

Science shares with art a concern for analysis to identify common patterns of form, structure and behaviour as well as relationships, reactions and changes of state. It requires us to use our senses to examine materials and the ways in which they change, for example when firing clay or setting plaster. Observation is central to all such tasks, a skill which needs training and practice. Looking is not enough. An activity involving words, measurement or reconstruction ensures that the observer gains some deeper understanding of whatever is being studied. Science requires children to have curiosity, which leads to investigation, experimentation and the ability to visualise, through the use of imagination, beyond what may be actually visible. Three-dimensional work is an ideal means of developing these attitudes and thinking skills.

Following a walk around the school grounds, a class of nine year olds produced models of trees or parts of trees. Their conversation during the walk was about the differences between trees. The children were given a choice of three-dimensional media with which they were familiar, to explore these differences. Clay proved to be a good way of studying branching and rooting structures, while wire or wire and plaster indicated the rhythm of branches typical to a particular tree.

To explore the relationship between animals and their environment, seven- and eight-year-old children made models of animals from soft wire and papier-mâché. These were placed in a landscape, made of card and scrap materials, which their research suggested would provide food and shelter.

Older children extended the exploration of environments by making undersea models using clay, which included fish and divers amongst rocks, weed and coral. Some suspended the fish on threads, others used wire to hold the fish above the sea bed. The questions raised with the children focussed on access to oxygen.

Making creatures with clay or wire offers a direct way for children to work out the details – the structure of components, how they fit together, how joints bend for movement – as well as the overall characteristics of the animal.

Physical education

A physical education lesson for nine year olds had the aim of making children more aware of the many ways in which their limbs can be used. They were faced with a series of obstacles (PE apparatus and heavy furniture) and they had to experiment with ways to cross, showing their ideas to each other and the teacher. This was followed immediately by making clay models of two or more figures crossing an obstacle, such as a fence, wall, cliff, or boulder. This resulted in discussion about the way joints bend. A longer-term outcome was evident in the drawings of some children who showed a greater understanding in their images when they came to draw people.

Music

Music can be an exciting stimulation to many kinds of creative work. Although some pieces of music can conjure up strong representational images, much is non-figurative. There are parallels with three-dimensional work, where the nature of the forms and textures produced reflects calmness or agitation, rhythm, movement or patterns for example. Contrasts which may occur in a piece of music can raise questions about the need for contrasts within a piece of sculpture.

Another area for exploitation is in making sounds by various means. Establishing the principle of a sound box can lead to experiments with stretching wires or strings along a board (see figure C33 on page 121 of the colour section). Taking a sound chamber such as an ocarina, the children can use clay to make variations of size and form to establish which works most successfully. Shaking, rattling and striking instruments are all also potentially worthwhile for children to explore. For this approach to succeed the children need to have access to, and prior experience of, a variety of materials so that they can select appropriately. Even more vital is their confidence to experiment, otherwise the work can become simple imitation of a given model.

Technology

The increasing emphasis which is being placed on technology in the curriculum opens up a wonderful range of experiences, many of which are closely linked to art and design. The nature of materials, their potentials and limitations, together with the processes and skills they require in use, are important things to learn. Designing, which raises issues of function, inventive thinking, visualising and aesthetics, challenges children by presenting them with the need to solve problems and make informed decisions (see figure C34 on page 121 of the colour section).

The core of most technology is the ability to visualise, which is a prime concern of three-dimensional work. Picturing structures and forms in the mind enables children to ask themselves many questions as they are working, about materials, relationships between parts, methods of forming or constructing.

> What would happen if . . . ? How would this look if . . . ? How can I make this part move . . . ? How can I make this stronger?

Many of the answers to these questions depend on the children having a sense of form and structure, which comes from regular experience in handling basic materials and tackling tasks (see figure 11a). The ability to identify needs, and to understand and solve

Figure 11a Constructing in thick paper (age 10)

problems successfully as a result of thinking and working out practical solutions for themselves, does not happen without planned progression of opportunities for children to work in this way.

Designing brings together these abilities with a feeling for the appearance – the aesthetics or visual rightness of the work – which is again developed through regular use of the visual elements. Behind all our teaching in technology there must be a concern for people and our surroundings. It is extremely important to encourage children to look at what they are making, or have made, and to discuss it critically. Helping children to find confidence in their own ideas, to try things out to see if they will work, and persevere through a number of trials and errors should be part of our supportive role as teachers. Designing is about making technology useful and acceptable (see figure 11b).

Figure 11b Inventing playground equipment in card and timber (age 9)

Many themes in education have no particular boundaries. Themes such as buildings, change, water and transport can easily spread with the use of a topic web until every aspect of the curriculum is involved. When this happens the teacher needs to select and focus on those parts which will be most effective in realising the aims of the topic. On many occasions I have seen models forming the centre piece for the work because of the way in which three-dimensional models can reveal information and stimulate understanding about matters in the world outside (see figure 11c).

Figure 11c Investigating different structures of bridges in card (age 10)

ENVIRONMENT AND ENVIRONMENTS

Study of environment only makes sense when it crosses subject boundaries. We can measure, describe verbally or by drawing, listen, smell, feel, or move around in order to absorb what is there. The geography, history and science of a particular place are revealed interdependently through activities central to art, by observation, analysis and recording the systems that operate within it.

Children must relate closely to their surroundings in order to understand the place they inhabit and for which they share responsibility. Books, television and computer technology provide children with exciting ways of learning and experiencing, but they need balancing with a substantial helping of reality. Two-dimensional images, including those concerned with constructing or giving the illusion of three dimensions, only offer a limited sense of the qualities of the actual materials, forms, structures and spaces of the real world.

Actively building life-sized environments of all kinds can be a rich educational experience as they allow children to be within what they have made. Parts of classrooms, playgrounds or school fields can be transformed into other places, ages, cultures or fantasy worlds.

A number of nationally and internationally recognised artists are working in and with the environment, for example Andy

Goldsworthy and Eduardo Paollozzi. They explore it in direct ways, reflecting on environmental issues and developing understanding about relationships between people and places. Some artists modify the natural state of things so that we become more aware of the qualities and wonders of the world. Others use industrial, commercial and domestic waste to transform debris into real art forms or to produce images which can be of great beauty, startling, threatening or disturbing.

Jan Marshall, an artist from Cumbria, uses natural materials to produce environments, reliefs, drawings and prints. She creates surfaces with leaves, twigs, nuts, stones, which are attached to boards with PVA resin and then varnished (see figure 12a). The results are thoroughly intriguing to touch as well as to the eye (with 'please touch' notices). Her environments, which she calls 'installations', are built with branches to suggest enclosed spaces like tunnels and caves, each with a different feeling (see figures 12b and c). Much of her art is about special 'magical' places. Children find this type of display particularly exciting, and many seem to understand and intuitively equate it with their own desire to create their special places in which to play, hide or fantasise. Using natural materials seems absolutely right for fulfilling such in-built instincts and feelings for the natural world.

Jan states:

> As a physically challenged artist, wheelchair user and also sufferer of a serious depressive illness, I have become aware of my own potential through art. The spaces I create make me feel good, positive, and I can see people becoming aware of their surroundings and own feelings, as they experience and explore the created installations. They take part which is, for the ordinary viewer, something very unusual but becomes very moving and memorable – special. I realise how my art has helped heal me and I believe the creation of such art can help heal others who take an active part in its creation, or simply discover its presence in passing.

Figure 12a *Touch canvas*, panel of stones and twigs, Jan Marshall

Figure 12b *Walk-in tent*, branches and natural materials, Jan Marshall

Figure 12c *Sweat lodge*, branches, cloth and candles, Jan Marshall

Clearly her art acts as a form of therapy for her, but the main motivation is her excitement with nature and the ideas she can fulfil through its use.

Location plays a big part in determining what resources are available to a school, especially when it is working with the outside environment, but even an apparently limited location such as an inner-city school surrounded by high-rise blocks can have something to offer. Resources in the locality of the school should be explored and exploited first and visits to places of particular richness planned and undertaken whenever possible. The techniques learned through local visits can then be applied with greater confidence and speed when moving further afield.

Some teachers arrange residential courses, providing a whole range of valuable cross-curricular, social and learning experiences. These have been a particularly fruitful part of my work with children and teachers for many years. Three days on one theme may seem optimistic in terms of application, but in practice the special circumstances of being in a new place and doing interesting practical activities, ensure that concentration is maintained. Whether the focus is on nature or architecture, initial looking and talking leads to the need to record observations, which may be by drawing, writing or tape recording, but equally can be done using clay, wire or plaster casting. Drawing may be preparation for making models, but equally three-dimensional models may be a way into understanding form and space so that it can be represented in two dimensions more accurately. These projects are rich in cross-curricular approaches.

Working in the environment is about direct sensory experiences: looking, touching, smelling and listening and so learning about the qualities of matter. It also involves questioning, classifying, grouping, rearranging, discriminating and enjoying the excitement and potential of the experience and resources available (see figure C35 on page 122 of the colour section).

Children can explore patterns and structures using material found in the environment, working individually or in groups, and using a variety of scales. I have worked in this way with fallen material in woodland, flotsam on the sea shore or building blocks and pieces of timber on a school playground.

Figure 13 Sea anemones modelled in clay, fired and glazed (age 11)

Themes may be abstract, exploiting the qualities of the materials, reflecting the patterns and structures to be found in the location, reorganising what exists. Alternatively the purpose could be the representation of figures or animals (see figure 13) or resolving design problems, for example making a seat, shelter, tunnel or maze. Where possible it is useful to record children's work photographically or on video, as sites usually have to be returned to their original state at the end of the project. This offers opportunities for communicating what has been done to other children, staff and parents.

Children must be made aware of the rules of ecology and conservation for any particular location. What is required on one site may differ from another. In many cases any fallen material which is not growing can be used. Some site owners may be pleased to have material removed, or the children's finished work can be left intact. Much depends on plans for the future of the site. The rules must be discussed with the owner or warden first, though my experience has been one of interest and encouragement, whether dealing with an undeveloped site or Forestry Commission property.

City centre playgrounds may seem unpromising, but I have seen some outstanding work produced by children as a result of looking in nooks and crannies at plant and insect life, using magnifyers and then constructing models on a large scale with canes, wire, string and paper. Another school persuaded a builder parent to bring in bricks, breeze blocks, planks and lengths of timber, which were used to create safe, low level structures and on one occasion, collectively design a more interesting playground, with seats, walkways, flower containers and play structures. This activity involved a great deal of discussion, cooperation, use of imagination and design thinking, model-making and drawing.

A group of 40 children, ten from each of a first, middle and secondary school and a sixth form, were gathered at a residential centre for three days. They were taken for a walk around the grounds looking for evidence of short- and long-term changes. They were then given an extensive choice of media in which to explore the theme of change: writing, photography, computers, video, drama and art activities which included work with clay, wire and plaster. Course members went back to the environment before deciding which aspect and what activities to select. Some older pupils used natural materials to produce patterns and images on the ground, and built structures, each demonstrating some aspect of the theme. Younger children watched, but soon joined in and created their own work (see figure 14a, and also figures C36, C37 and C38 on pages 122 and 123 of the colour section). Later work included taking impressions of tree bark, weathered brickwork and a decaying tree stump, using clay and plaster casts (see page 82). The children also made models in clay of buildings as they used to be (see figure 14b), or as they could become (there was an interesting ruin in the grounds), and wire and plaster studies of trees.

Three-dimensional work gives direct access to many facets of our surroundings. Looking at the work of artists and designers can focus and extend our vision even further. No matter where we live we can find a variety of locations worthy of study and artists, designers and craftworkers, who can enrich our understanding of what is there. It is from the environment that many of our most useful resources originate, whether it is subject matter to study or materials with which to work.

Figure 14a Arrangement of leaves (age 8)

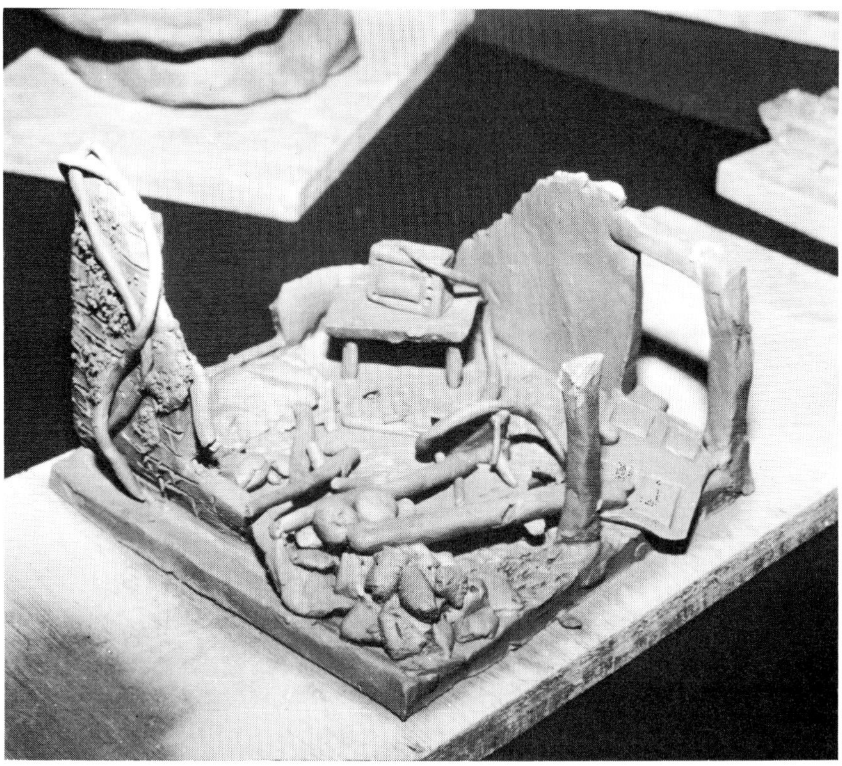

Figure 14b Ruin, made from clay slabs and developed by modelling (age 10)

3 Resources: materials, tools and equipment

BASIC EXPERIENCES

The act of handling and exploring a variety of malleable and rigid materials provides the most basic means of learning and one which children quite naturally gravitate towards, if they are given the opportunity. We only need to consider the way children (and adults!) play with sand, water, textured items and textiles to realise that this is a powerful way in which we find out about the qualities and behaviour of the 'ingredients' of the world (see figure C39 on page 124 of the colour section). Investigating contrasting qualities such as hardness and softness, roughness or smoothness, rigidity or flexibility, toughness or friability, as well as being enjoyable, builds up knowledge so that appropriate materials can be chosen for particular tasks. Appreciating these qualities and using their potential is something we all need in order to enrich our lives and solve some of the practical problems we face. It is this natural progression from exploration to experimentation which naturally leads to children developing their own ideas.

Making things involves developing confidence, and understanding what materials will really do. In some cases this means accepting their traditional use but in other situations it means breaking new ground where the only rules are those needed for safety. Finding the limitations of materials, as well as their potential, can be a valuable learning experience.

Practically all the materials we use in three-dimensional work have their origins in the environment. Some are in their natural state, others modified or treated to make them usable, while a few are the result of physical or chemical processing. This suggests that we should collect some materials outside, and indeed this can be an excellent way of helping children understand the nature of matter and where it comes from. In practice, time often does not allow us to take the children outside, for example to dig and clean our own clay, as a regular activity, but great value can be derived from occasional excursions of this kind. Collecting natural materials such as branches, leaves, stones and shells, or suitable manufacturer's waste such as packaging, timber off-cuts, or plastic mouldings, can provide rich sources for constructing and making. Earth, sand and more transient resources from our surroundings such as water, plant material or snow, can produce other forms of work. Anyone who has seen Andy Goldsworthy's exciting ice and snow sculptures and collections of arranged leaves, bark and other natural items will realise that this whole area of experience can be one of great depth, skill and beauty. This raises questions as to whether the work needs to be permanent, indestructable or whether the changes of state provide an extra quality to the creative experience. I believe that there are times when it is right to take work through a number of stages to a final product which can be saved and enjoyed, but there are also many learning experiences producing impermanent results, which can be equally valuable.

Whilst the possible range of materials and tools for three-dimensional work can be very wide I believe that it is important to concentrate on basics. Children only learn to handle and control a medium by using it many times, and although there can be excitement in a constant introduction of new materials, there is seldom development.

I am therefore concentrating on the following materials, and the tools and processes they involve:

Clay
Other malleable materials
Wire
Plaster
Constructional materials, including timber, metals, plastics, paper and card and natural materials
Papier-mâché

CLAY

Clay is one of the most versatile malleable materials for giving children rich three-dimensional experiences. It has an immediacy in its response to young fingers and the capacity for change at great speed. The ease of transforming the clay from one shape to another by manipulating it in their hands means that children can explore possibilities and ideas rapidly (see figures 15a and b, and also figure

C40 on page 124 of the colour section). Further adjustment and modification can be made by adding or removing clay. Handling a responsive material can, in itself, provide a stimulation to mental creativity. In addition it can be used in many technically different ways, such as modelling, constructing, carving and casting.

Figure 15a Manipulating clay (age 6)

Figure 15b Creatures modelled in clay (age 5 to 6)

In an educational context I prefer the term 'clay work' rather than 'pottery' in order to suggest that there are many different uses for clay other than pots and that it need not always be fired. Having the facility to fire clay is, however, an advantage as it provides a way of making items permanent and allows children to experience the changes of state brought about by firing and glazing (see figure C41 on page 125 of the colour section).

There is so much to be learned through working with clay that even without a kiln it can be a rich experience. Exploration and experimentation, and seeing what the clay can and cannot do by squeezing, pushing and pulling, are all useful experiences (see figure C42 on page 125 of the colour section). Often children move on to develop their ideas by building up shapes and models (see figures C43 and C44 on pages 125 and 126 of the colour section). Spindly details and poorly joined pieces may well break off as the clay dries, and children quickly learn what has happened in discussion and make adjustments in later work. Building models on a sturdy clay base can reduce the risk of broken extremities for unfired work. Indeed the base can be an advantage in that it encourages the children to put the model in context, for example, by setting an animal in its own environment.

Surfaces may be textured, smoothed or imprinted and need not be coloured or taken further – in fact they often look better if left at this stage. Unfired pieces can have their surfaces treated in a variety of ways, by burnishing (rubbing with the back of a spoon), polishing with wax or shoe polish, varnishing with PVA medium or varnish. A coat of thinned PVA can reduce absorbency so that water-based paints can be applied to give the work colour.

Choosing clays

There are many clays available, each with different qualities of colour, texture and firing temperature. Most are mixtures designed to fulfil particular needs.

Grog (which is clay which has been fired and then pulverised) is a common additive. Grogs are graded according to particle size to give different textures and structural properties to the clays.

Two clays of contrasting qualities, one coarse and one smoother and of a different colour, cover most educational needs.

Pink crank mixture, which has a coarse grog content, is ideal for large modelling and constructional work with children of all ages. The large particles in the clay ensure that the steam can escape readily, so that large, solid pieces can be fired if necessary. It also means that water is absorbed quickly when dry clay has to be reclaimed for further use.

Grey modelling or **school clay** is often called 'buff' because of its colour when fired. This usually has a fine grog addition and some form of this clay is available from most suppliers. This clay is ideal for fine detail when modelling, constructing or casting.

Oxidising St Thomas' body is another useful clay, less coarse in texture than crank mixture but of similar colour.

Storing clay

Storing clay in use is best done in sturdy plastic bins fitted with lids. A piece of polythene pressed to the exposed surface of the clay reduces evaporation. Regular checking, and sprinkling with water if necessary, ensures that the clay is always ready for use. A bin over 60 cm high is more easily moved around the classroom if it is on a bin 'dolly', which is a platform on wheels, available from educational suppliers. There are purpose-made sturdy, rectangular containers with close fitting lids and wheels fixed to the base available too. Long-term storage of bags of clay should be away from heaters. Outside is fine, as frost will do no harm.

Preparing clay

New clay can be used straight from the package, which is normally a polythene bag. Clay which has been used before may need a light spraying with water to restore its consistency. With the 'open' (grogged) clays I use, the water soaks in quite quickly. A few seconds of kneeding consolidates the clay and helps the plasticity. Clay which is in a poor, uneven state, may need more thorough treatment on the same lines, but should additionally be wedged. This means cutting the lump of clay vertically into two pieces and with one piece on a solid surface, thumping the other hard on top of it to drive out air pockets; this should be repeated once or twice. It is best done on a solid surface, such as the floor, and if a table is used, it should be done directly over a table leg. As little time as possible should be spent on this as there are more important things to do. A clay cutter helps distribute pieces from a large block of clay quickly.

Reclaiming clay

Unfired clay can be used over and over again as long as it keeps its plasticity. Break dry clay into small pieces and soak it in a bucket of water until it is of an even consistency. Then spread it thickly on a board, paving slab, or best of all on a plaster slab outside, if possible in the sun or wind, turning and then kneading the clay from time to time until it feels ready for use, that is, easily malleable but not sticky.

Firing

Work to be fired must be thoroughly dry, which can take two days for small, thin items but a week for larger models. If, when you look underneath, there is a darker patch on the clay, the work needs to dry a little longer. Placing work near radiators, a firing kiln or in the sun can speed up the drying, but tiles or models with a flat base can distort if they are dried too quickly. If possible tiles should be turned over each day. To slow down the rate of drying, cover the work loosely with polythene.

Models made with smoother clays may have to be hollowed so that no part is more than 1.5 cm thick if the work is to be fired. Hollowing should be done when the clay is partially dry (a state called 'leather hard', which is self-explanatory) using a wire tool or, for slender parts, a pencil or shaped stick. A drill bit, twisted with fingers, can be useful to produce the required air channels.

Dry ware can be stacked onto the kiln shelves; items can touch, provided they are not glazed and flat tiles can be placed in piles to save space. Ware must not touch the sides of the kiln. The temperature for firing should be raised gradually at first to allow the water, in the form of steam, to escape slowly, which also means leaving the bung hole of the kiln open. This can be done overnight. Once a temperature of 600° C has been reached the temperature rise can be faster. For the first firing, also known as bisque or biscuit, a temperature of 960° C is normally sufficient. At this temperature the kiln can be switched off and allowed to cool slowly overnight before opening the door. Cracking or splitting could occur if the door is opened too soon.

For glaze firing the ware must be cleaned of glaze underneath and placed on specially made stilts so that it does not touch the kiln shelf or other pieces of work. Firing can be a little quicker with the bung hole closed and the final temperature should be within the range specified on the glaze package. Gradual cooling is important once more.

Clay equipment

Setting up for clay work need not be expensive. Tools may be bought but most can be made from readily available bits and pieces:

Baseboards pieces of hardboard, plywood or blockboard in assorted sizes.
Modelling tools purchased as 'boxwood tools', or 10–15 cm

lengths of dowel or twig with shaped ends. Old kitchen knives, forks, large screws, nails, plastic items, pieces of broken hacksaw blade and so on, can also be useful.

Rolling pins and guides or pieces of broomhandle and 0.5 to 1.5 cm strips of wood.

Hessian or polythene on which to roll slabs of clay.

Clay cutter a 50 cm length of thin wire or fishing line with a toggle on each end.

Slab cutter or 'harp' These can be purchased or made from a length of mild steel rod or tube, about 80 cm long, bent into a shallow U so that the sides are about 20 cm long. The arms are notched with a hacksaw at 3 mm intervals for 5 cm from each end, and pieces of thin wire or thick fishing line are stretched tightly between corresponding notches, so that they can be adjusted to the required thickness of clay. (Figure 31 on page 78 shows the harp in use.)

Wire tools for hollowing work can be made from dowel with a wire loop lashed on the end.

Polythene thin, to keep the models damp.

Whirlers or banding wheels enable models to be rotated easily, thereby encouraging consideration of all sides of 3-D work. Not essential.

Plastic lidded bins for clay storage and reclaiming.

Kilns already to be found in many primary schools. Firing is not difficult, in fact kilns are easier to use than some domestic ovens! Health and safety regulations must, of course, be carefully implemented.

Slips and glazing

Traditional techniques of making and firing forms, and colouring and glazing surfaces have a good deal of value in the educational experiences of young children. Children should have the opportunity to appreciate and make use of these whenever possible (see figure C45 on page 126 of the colour section).

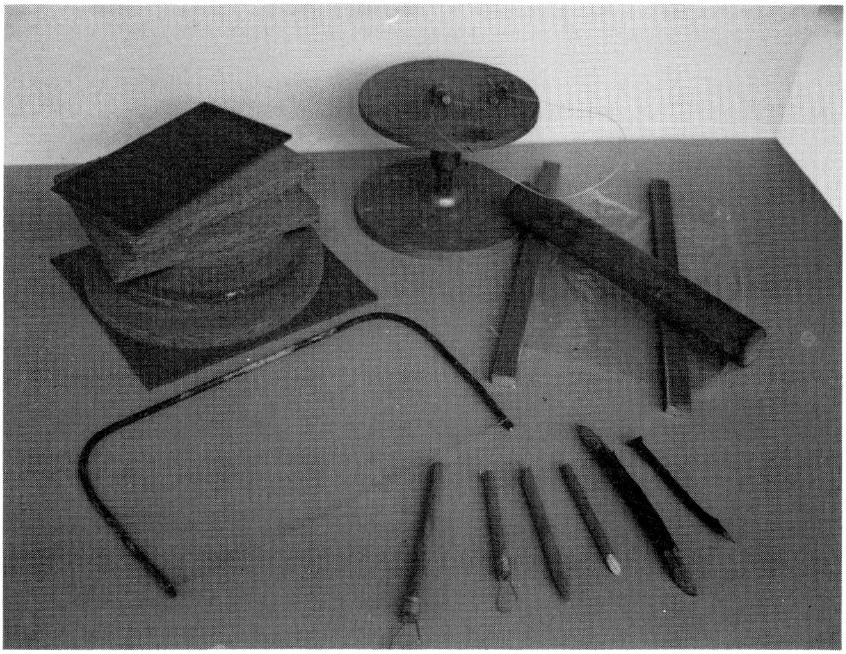

Figure 16 Clay equipment

Slip is liquid clay of a creamy consistency, which is applied to the model while still damp by dipping, brushing thickly or 'trailing' (like piping icing on a cake) with a plastic or rubber syringe. Colouring agents, which are mostly derived from metallic oxides, can be mixed with slips to give a good range of colours which have a natural quality. Metallic oxides, in common with all chemicals, must be handled with care and children using them closely supervised, as many of them can be harmful if ingested.

Glaze is a layer of glass closely integrated with the surface of the clay. Children like the shiny quality of glazed work and where a kiln is available, using and developing a range of glazes can be a fascinating and never-ending exploration.

Glazes are supplied as powders, which are a combination of chemicals. They are mixed at the approximate ratio of 1 kilo of powder to 1 litre of water and stirred thoroughly to form a suspension. The exact consistency depends on the porosity of the models to be glazed, which in turn depends on the temperature at which the clay has been fired. The higher the temperature, the less porous the clay will be. To test the mix, dip a piece of once-fired clay into the mix for five to ten seconds. When removed it should dry in seconds and look as though it has an even coat of emulsion paint on the surface. If the glaze looks thick or lumpy, add more water; if it runs off leaving a very thin coating, allow the glaze to settle overnight and pour off some of the water. The glaze must be thoroughly mixed every time it is used to ensure that the suspension gives a balance of the constituent chemicals.

Glazes are usually applied by dipping work which has been fired into the glaze, but in recent years, brush-on glazes have been developed which can be painted directly and thickly onto the surface.

I recommend using a leadless transparent glaze with a gloss finish, firing at a temperature between 1050° and 1150° C, and possibly a white opaque zircon glaze with a gloss finish firing in the same range, as this makes firing simpler. Adding one or two coloured glazes can extend possibilities for older children. Buy small quantities and test the colour before placing a larger order.

Most slips and glazes are a shade of grey when in their fluid state, which makes it difficult for young children to visualise what the fired colour will be. A sample of the colour on a small clay tile tied to the handle or neck of each container helps children to know what to expect when the work is fired.

In other situations it may be more appropriate to use non-traditional or simpler, direct methods to colour or glaze. For example, a young child modelling a section of landscape may require colour to identify the different parts in a way which is far too complex to be fulfilled by glazes or pottery pigments. Waiting for a week or so for drying and firing can see the evaporation of interest for the young. The immediate answer may be to apply liquid or powder paint with slightly diluted PVA medium. Though this is not a ceramic technique, it deals with the educational needs of the moment.

OTHER MALLEABLE MATERIALS

There are a number of alternative materials which can be manipulated by children, each with its own properties.

Dough provides a good, slightly elastic material which can be squeezed, rolled and cut into shapes and forms. It is made by mixing 250 g of flour with 125 g of salt and then adding about 200 ml of water, a little at a time to give a firm consistency. Models can be baked in a moderate oven for an hour or so, after which they can be painted and varnished with PVA medium if required.

Plasticine can be hard for little fingers to manipulate unless it is very new or warmed, but is convenient for small tasks and available in an attractive range of colours.

A number of **self-hardening clays** have been developed over the years, some of which can be hardened in a domestic oven, while others require an additive. They tend to be much more expensive than normal clays and some have a texture which is less malleable and sensitive in handling.

WIRE

The properties of wire open up many exciting possibilities for older primary age children. Wire provides a rigid support for models which are to be made from plaster, fabrics, papier-mâché or, for temporary work, clay. (Clay shrinks as it dries but the wire does not, so cracking occurs.) Working with wire can be thought of as drawing in three dimensions, using the linear quality of wire for its own sake. This can enable children to explore or analyse the nature of many kinds of structures, natural or made. All kinds of ideas and sizes of work can be developed, from individual, hand-held models to huge structures built by a group for use in drama or as a project centre-piece.

There are several useful types of wire readily available, the cheapest of which is the galvanised iron used on farms or in gardens, which can be bought from most garden centres or hardware stores in coils. This wire is reasonably springy, does not rust (therefore plaster is not stained), and is available in a variety of thicknesses. I use three thicknesses for most teaching situations: one of 2.5 mm to give rigidity, one of 1.5 mm for small scale work or infilling and a binding wire of 0.5 to 0.75 mm.

In contrast, florists' wire is of black iron and has a very 'dead' feel to it, retaining exactly whatever shape it is manipulated into, which makes it very easy for 'drawing'. This wire is usually supplied in cut lengths of about 30 cm, is 2 mm thick, and can be obtained from florists' suppliers or some florists' shops. It rusts if wet, so is not suitable for use with plaster.

Alloy wires tend to be expensive, are soft and easy to manipulate, with little spring. For some work with children I have stripped off-cuts of cables and flex to get copper-wire, which is attractive in colour and easy to handle.

Plastic-coated garden wire is useful but expensive. One school found a skip full of telephone wire, which was thin, plastic covered and in a range of colours. The children used this as a modelling material, squeezing a mass of wire into the forms of people and animals.

Undoing coils of springy wire can catch and hurt the unwary. It is safer to cut coils into manageable lengths of 1 m or less, before giving it to children. Where space is tight I also double over about 0.5 cm at the end of each length to reduce the risk of scratches, until the children are used to handling the material and can prepare it for themselves.

Cutting wire (hide the scissors!) requires sidecutting pliers, which combine cutting edges with surfaces for gripping the wire.

Some structures may need a base board to give the work stability. Bending thick wire twice at right angles and nailing or stapling it to a piece of ply, block or chipboard gives a secure start. If the wire is used as a support for clay or plaster, it is essential that allowance is made for the weight of material it will have to support. A collapsing model can be a time-wasting problem!

Wire mesh, or chicken wire, is available from hardware stores or garden centres and has many possibilities, either for giving support to other materials or as a means of describing surfaces in wire models. Whether used in conjunction with timber or wire structures or on its own, the mesh formation allows it to be bent, crumpled, stretched or pushed into shape. Cutting requires a pair of snips or pliers and a little patience as it has to be cut strand by strand. Children should be advised to take care of the cut ends. Turning the points back on themselves, like a hem, removes the scratchy ends. Useful mesh sizes are between 2.5 cm and 5 cm.

PLASTER

Working with plaster can be an exciting experience for children, provided that the activity is well organised. The way that plaster changes, from powder to 'cream', from 'cheese' to 'stone' as the chemical reaction takes place, can be fascinating in itself. Initially most plaster sets in a few minutes to form a hard substance, then it continues to harden steadily over several days as water evaporates from the surface. It can be used for modelling, casting and carving and may be used in conjunction with other materials.

There are many kinds of plaster available, all with different properties, for example speed of setting, hardness and texture. Those in common use in the building industry can be used but tend to be coarse and less attractive in colour compared to other kinds. For most purposes I use fine white plaster (Plaster of Paris) which is inexpensive and obtainable from most builders' merchants. Very similar is potters' plaster, available from pottery suppliers.

Fine white plaster is mixed by putting an appropriate volume of water in a plastic container (empty margarine cartons are ideal) and sprinkling the dry powder into the water. Mix in the ratio of approximately 850 g of powder to 0.5 litres of water. Do not stir until practically the whole of the water has become sludge, which can be seen by tilting the container from side to side. A little mountain will build up in the centre. By not stirring, air is allowed to escape so that the particles of plaster are in direct contact with the water. This ensures that the chemical reaction will take place fully. When all the powder is in the water and it has stood for a minute or so, it can be stirred, hands being the best tool as you can feel when the mix is even. Other plasters may require different ways of mixing.

Plasters set at different speeds according to their type and condition, some in a few minutes, others in half an hour. It is wisest to test the setting time and condition of each batch before use. Some deterioration may be expected with time, which means that the chemical reaction will not take place fully and so the work stays soft or powdery. A damp hand, spillage of water or poor storage may have affected the powder. Once this has happened, it should be thrown away.

Using small containers controls the quantity being mixed; bucketfuls are difficult to handle and can be wasteful if they set more quickly than they can be used. All waste plaster, including scrapings from hands, tools and containers, must be put into bins and not washed down sinks.

I frequently use short lengths of cotton or jute (hessian), scrim (from builders' merchants, used by plasterers to cover joins in plasterboard), or similar open woven material, or even strips of newspaper, dipped in plaster and draped across a support to create surfaces. Modroc is a plaster-impregnated bandage which is use to set broken limbs, and which is dipped in water and used in a similar way, but it is more expensive. Spatulas, plastic palette knives, spoons or kitchen knives are useful for handling and modelling the setting plaster. Hacksaw blades are particularly useful once the plaster begins to set. The plaster can be carved, scraped, sawn or filed to refine its form, though the quality of a directly modelled surface is often more appropriate and attractive.

Plaster models which have dried for a day or more should be sprayed with water before any more plaster is added to the surface. Dry plaster is very absorbent and will draw the water out of applied plaster before the chemical change has taken place, resulting in a loose, powdery surface. Plaster casts can be washed under a tap and brushed to remove any bits of clay adhering to the surface. Once set the plaster will not dissolve.

It is important to keep clay which has been used for any work involving plaster separate from that which might be used for fired ware, as particles of plaster can shatter clay in the kiln, and will usually destroy the model.

Carving plaster can be very worthwhile for older primary children who are producing forms which are representational or exploring aesthetically pleasing shapes and surfaces. I find it helpful for children to start by carving blocks of clay to establish the idea of releasing a shape from within the block. This avoids the total demolition of plaster blocks! Plastic trays divided with strips of hardboard are ideal for producing the plaster blocks. The strips can be arranged irregularly so that the children can select the shape and size they want to carry out their idea. Blocks made in the morning can be carved in the afternoon while they have the consistency of cheese, using kitchen knives. As the plaster sets and dries and becomes harder over a period of two weeks, the tools may change to include rasps and at the end sandpaper or even hands for polishing the surface.

CONSTRUCTIONAL MATERIALS

Rigid materials of many kinds, including timber blocks and strips of various thicknesses, sheet materials, rods, plastic off-cuts or

gure 17 Sitting figure made
om packaging (age 6)

mouldings, soft metal rods and sheet, boxes and all manner of bits and bobs can be explored for their constructional possibilities. They can be combined with string, tape or fabrics if required. All can be added to clay, plaster and wire, which can also play a major part in providing constructional experiences.

Every primary school I visit uses packaging and scrap materials, readily available at little or no cost. A box is one of the most basic elements – unmodified it may become a car, boat, den, hiding place or whatever imagination requires. Several boxes can be grouped or piled to create other structures or environments and extend the possibilities (see figure 17).

Much can be done with a single box of any size by using paint and collage, though it may be necessary to glue paper to the sides to give a surface suitable for paint.

Scrap material can be used at any age in order to represent many possible themes, from animals to buildings, boats to machines, and so on. Card tubes from drapers or carpet stores, sawn into suitable lengths, all kinds of packaging and off-cuts of softwood all add to the variety of shapes and forms to be exploited (see figures 18 and 19).

Straws, pipe cleaners, strip wood, dowels, balsa wood and many other items are produced for the educational market and each has its

Figure 18 Design for a car, made from packaging and scrap material (age 10)

Figure 19 Figure constructed from scrap materials, plaster and paint (age 11)

use. Rolled paper tubes, thin strips of wood, wire and string can fulfil most of the same needs. Saw mills, builders and DIY stores can be sources of timber off-cuts which can be cut into convenient blocks or lengths for the children to use. Building blocks and bricks are heavy to handle but can be used for ground level work, say not more than three units high. Plastic pipes or tubes can be sawn into short cylinders or kept as long lengths. Ropes, builders' heavy duty polythene, garden canes, tree branches and twigs can all present exciting possibilities for working outside or indoors. String and wire are useful for making joints in constructional work which involves branches, sticks or canes.

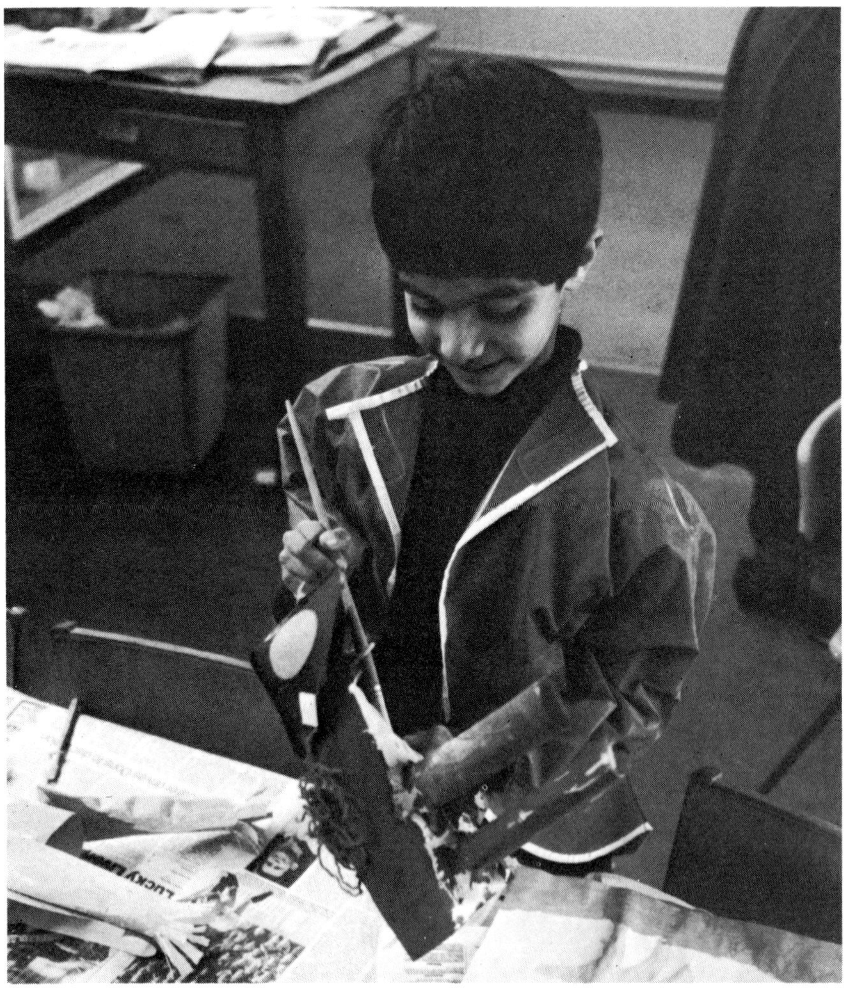

Figure 20 Painting a boat constructed from card (age 6)

Tools for constructional work could include small saws such as 'pad' saws, hand drills, a vice to hold work securely for cutting or drilling, hammers and nails, and a glue gun for older pupils.

Paper and card

Much paper and card can be obtained by collecting packaging and off-cuts from around the school, from printing works and, for thicker card, from picture framers (see figure 20). Quite small pieces can still be used for constructional work. Card can be bought reasonably cheaply, and I find Manilla board to be one of the most useful. Older children who have been carefully instructed can cut it with good scissors or craft knives and it is easy to score and fold.

Young children may need some help when cutting paper and card. Good quality scissors can cope with most situations and can be used to score paper or card in order to get a good fold. Eventually, with older children, small craft knives become more versatile, allowing them to cut complex shapes. Knives should be used on a cutting board, such as a piece of hardboard or a plastic cutting mat, with a steel safety rule, i.e. one with a raised centre and a channel for giving a firm, safe grip.

Deciding on the age when knives can be used is a matter of knowing the children, their sense of responsibility and manual control. Close adult supervision is essential and there must reasonable space around each child.

Adhesives

Sticking some materials together can be a problem as there is no safe glue to deal with every situation. I usually remove items which are difficult to stick from the collected materials. Plastic pots and waxed boxes are particularly difficult, but can be used in other ways or for other purposes. PVA adhesive in small plastic pots, applied with spreaders or strips of card, deals with most needs, supplemented with paper clips and fasteners, brown gumstrip and sticky tape. Sticking paper calls for cellulose or starch wallpaper paste (without fungicide). For exceptional situations where everything might be working well for a child apart from a particular joint, I keep tubes of specialised (though safe) glues, such as Copydex or resin wood glue, and a stapler, in my desk.

PAPIER-MÂCHÉ

Traditionally papier-mâché means soaking small pieces of absorbent paper (such as newspaper) in water until they become a pulp, which, mixed with paste, can be used as a modelling material. In the classroom I find it easier for children to use strips of paper, dipped into a bowl of starch or cellulose paste, then laid onto a support. The paper is built up in layers according to the size and strength required, usually between three and five thicknesses. It helps children to see when they have completed a layer if they alternate a layer of newspaper with one of coloured tissue paper. Screwed up dry paper or lumps of pulp can extend the modelling possibilities (see figure 21). Models can be supported by chicken wire, or a wire or timber armature, which become an integral part of the work. Where the piece needs to be lightweight a shaped piece of clay, a pile of damp sand, or even crumpled paper, may be a quicker and more suitable support, which can be removed when the work is dry.

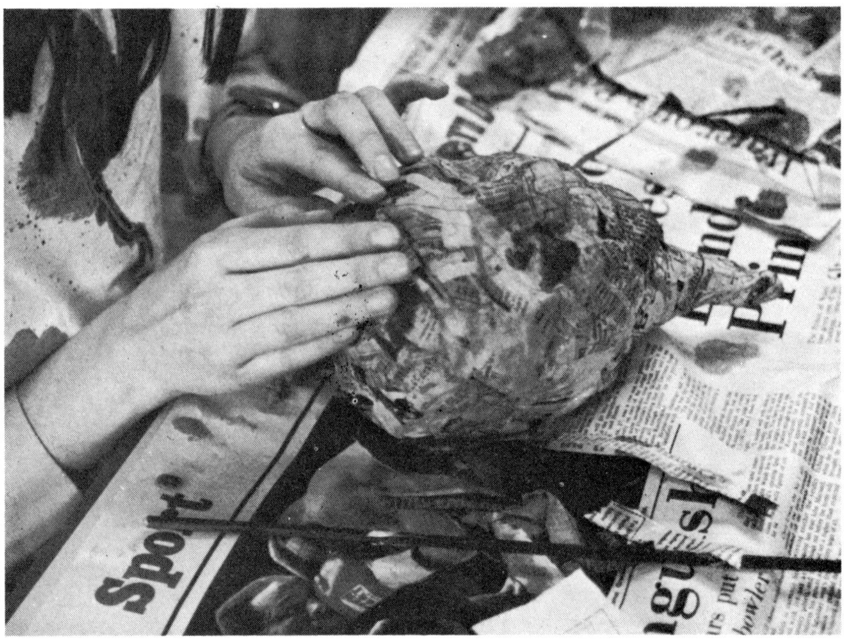

Figure 21 Papier-mâché head on a core of crumpled paper (age 11)

When dry, papier-mâché can be painted with any kind of paint (see figure 22), then varnished with PVA medium if a shiny surface is required. For large structures which may be used out of doors two coats of emulsion paint produce a very hard and durable surface, capable of withstanding heavy rain.

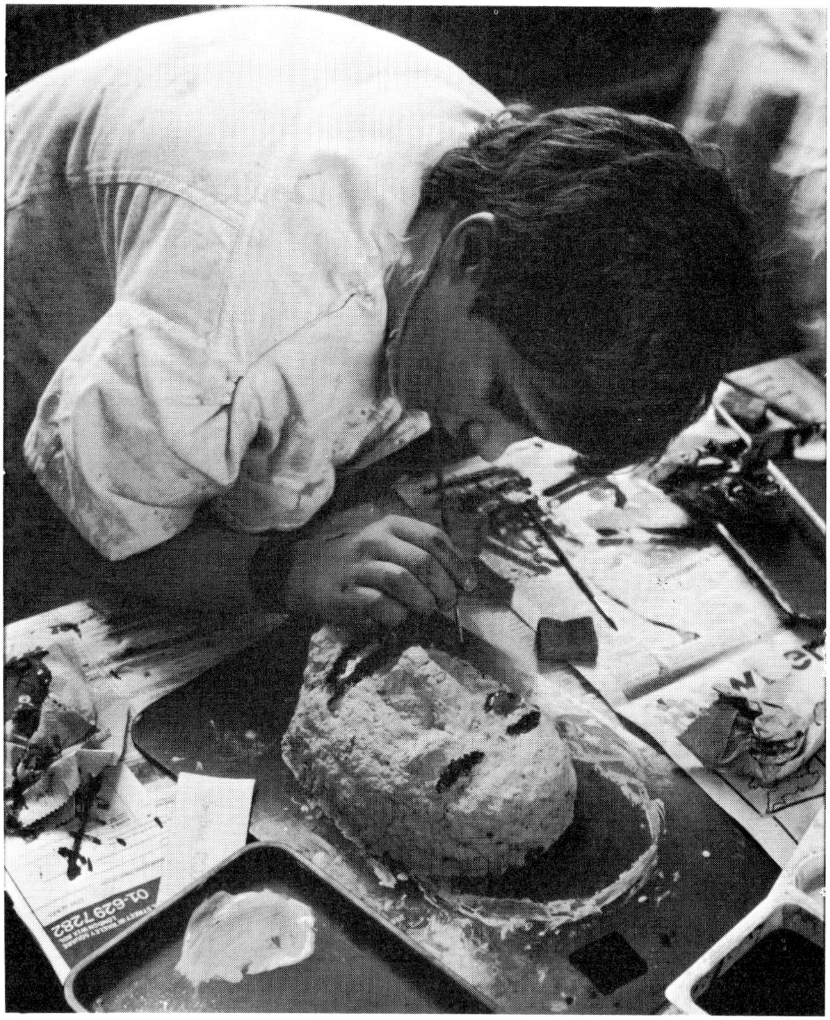

Figure 22 Painting papier-mâché (age 11)

WORKS OF ART, CRAFT AND DESIGN

Most schools have used art and design education as a largely practical subject, concerned with the children's own ideas and interpretations. In recent years there has been an exciting and productive growth in the use of work by adult artists, designers and craftworkers as stimulation, thematic and technical reference, for developing cultural awareness and as a source of enjoyment.

The National Curriculum has responded to this productive development positively and requires that:

pupils should understand and appreciate art in a variety of genres and styles from a variety of cultures.

Reproductions of work in books, teaching packs, photographs, slides and videos are readily available from publishers, museums and galleries. (The Contact Gallery in Norwich produces videos of each artist that exhibits there.) However, children need to realise that reproductions are limited and show only some of the qualities of the actual works, especially three-dimensional items. All-round viewing is essential to appreciate the forms, spaces, surface qualities and scale. Unless children have regular experiences of looking at the real thing, representations will not mean very much.

School and classroom displays, where items can be handled and viewed, provide a rich educational resource. Teachers, children and parents can be a good source of material for study. Many will have domestic or collected items which can be brought into the classroom. The cultural mix to be found in most schools can make this particularly rewarding.

Visiting galleries and museums should be part of every child's experience, and many such places have education officers who can guide and support the children with information and talks. These experiences can be extended by visits to suitable shops, as these can be good places to look at aspects of design – in products, packaging, store layout, and so on. There are shops which specialise in gathering work from across the world, which can be used to raise cultural, moral and ethical questions.

Going out for regular educational visits is important as a means of making education relevant to the children, but it may be difficult to cover all their needs in this way. I have used a variety of approaches to ensure that the children get to see works of art, craft and design frequently. Local studio potters, furniture makers and sculptors have been pleased to lend work and in some cases have visited the school to set up a display or to talk with the children about their work.

Some of the richest experiences for children have come from artists doing their own work in the school and being available for discussion with the children over a number of days. Some local and regional art associations have schemes for these projects and I have also had worthwhile collaborations with art colleges who gave students a period to work in schools. Artists and students have to be selected with care to ensure that the experience will be relevant to the children. Advice may be sought from the appropriate association or local authority.

Selecting suitable resources which fit in with the planned curriculum is important, but we should also capitalise on opportunities which may arise to give the children very special, but isolated experiences.

4 Teaching approaches

Children and teachers who can share interests and enthusiasms, whose ideas and opinions are mutually valued, are together likely to ensure successful education. Add to this the satisfaction which children get from producing tangible items and we have the potential for developing attitudes of confidence and commitment, where children are prepared to experiment, make decisions and take initiatives. Teachers need to consider how these attitudes and abilities can be fostered.

Initial planning of lessons clearly has to take into account the previous experiences of the children, the ways they are used to working, and their stage of development. On the other hand, children can be very adaptable and responsive to new opportunities if they have confidence and interest. Often the availability of space, tools and equipment means that a class has to have two or more activities going on simultaneously. This allows the teacher to concentrate on a group which is tackling a new or more complex task and, in a more detached way, to observe those operating with familiar tasks. As the groups change in the course of time, so every child gets the opportunity to work both closely with the teacher and independently.

CHILDREN'S NEEDS AND DEVELOPMENT

Every child has a different range of mental and physical potentials, develops at a variable pace and, if allowed, responds to situations in individual ways. Many of the developmental needs of children are common, but the exceptional are also our concern.

Just as there are broad, identifiable stages of development to be seen in children's two-dimensional work, so three-dimensional structures and forms also illustrate their level of development. Young children use symbols to represent objects, to convey ideas and information. These symbols become more sophisticated the more children use them and the more their knowledge increases. They may continue to use them as a convenient vocabulary for several years. Some children begin to work in a more visually responsive way before others. Whether this is sooner or later is of little importance. What matters is the quality of their thinking as indicated in their ability to produce ideas and responses for themselves.

Children who are unused to malleable materials may use them to 'draw' flat images at first, perhaps using 'worms' as lines, but usually move quickly on to solid forms, for example, a sphere on which facial features are drawn by scratching or incision. Later, features may be shown by increasingly detailed additions to the surface. If children have had the opportunity to manipulate the medium before, they will form some parts by moulding or pushing cavities into the mass.

The proportions or relative size of parts are often more accurate when working in the round rather than on paper, perhaps because children find it easier to identify the reality of solid forms with the actual subject. They have to work out how things fit together, determine spatial relationships, and construct their model so that it stands up in a way that may be less necessary for their drawings. This suggests that drawing and modelling can complement each other. Our task as teachers is to be aware of the way children's understanding of two- and three-dimensional images develops and changes. We are then in a position to support and encourage children in taking the next step, instead of imposing ways of learning that are beyond their capability, and which can result in children resorting to mechanical imitation rather than understanding what they are doing.

One of the best ways of getting children to develop their images, and to observe and think for themselves, is for them to produce more than one item (for example a person, head, animal, tree, building, or non-figurative model), either as a group, or separately, where the task is to compare or show differences. Contrasting two forms can move children on from producing all-embracing symbols, towards work which includes particular characteristics of the individual subjects. In the early years the task should be broad, showing the difference between a large and small animal, two people who do different jobs, or two buildings. Later the differences should be more subtle, as with dogs of different breeds, people sitting on a bench, or two shops where different things are sold. Relationships of all kinds can be explored to contrast characteristics, for example a mother or father and child, a group of friends, families, human figures, playing musical instruments or a person with an animal. Visual evidence of emotions such as affection or anger, happiness or sorrow can further extend the potentials for comparison.

ENCOURAGING CHILDREN TO WORK CREATIVELY

The essential aspect of all creative activity is that the children should have the opportunity to respond to materials, to think and work creatively themselves. In order to do this there may be a need for the children to have practical experience supported by technical information, building up basic skills. For most three-dimensional work these are straightforward and need very little time. The development of most practical skills can be an integral part of the creative activity.

Working creatively brings together a whole range of prior experiences, knowledge, thinking skills and the confidence to select ideas and materials, make decisions and visualise possibilities through imagination and fantasy. Throughout, the teacher has a vital role of support, encouragement and stimulation.

It is important to establish when children need information, instruction, demonstration, when close support and encouragement is required and when it is better to stand well back and give children the opportunity to think and work things out for themselves.

Information about technical matters or safety needs to be explicit. Where a sequence of operations is involved, the order has to be established clearly. When joining clay the children need an explanation of the way in which damp clay may stick together on contact but will fall apart when dry. Joining wire, mixing plaster, using a craft knife, for example, are all techniques needing a simple demonstration to ensure success. I prefer to avoid showing more than is absolutely necessary and never produce a finished result, so that the children have something to discover.

Children may require discussion, stimulating experiences or access to reference material when starting a new theme or idea. Exploration of materials may call for a certain amount of encouragement to begin with, but should lead to freedom for individual discovery. When the groundwork has been established and the children are equipped to explore, the teacher can stand back, giving them time to think and make their own decisions. For some, who have not had the privilege of working independently before, it may be necessary to explain that the teacher, though in the room, has reading to listen to, marking to do, or a cupboard to be reorganised, so that the children have to be self-reliant for a period. Observing children in this slightly detached way can supply useful information about their capability. It is also helpful in identifying where there is real need for support.

Some important types of work, where the aim is to get the children to respond instinctively and spontaneously to an experience, require a different approach. The starting point could be from some special experience by one or more of the children, a poem, drama activity, or an object or creature brought into the classroom. In such cases I prefer the children to use media with which they feel confident, so that their thinking and action can focus on their responses.

A new material can be a source of considerable curiosity and excitement for the children, so it is important to show it to the whole class and to ensure that they all have an opportunity to try it out in turn. If you are introducing a new process which requires close supervision to one group at a time, it may be better for the rest of the class to be involved with simple, familiar processes but new subject matter.

There are some situations where it is necessary for the teacher to set a very specific, communal theme or task – for example modelling heads, making ceremonial masks, making a clay box or cylinder, or making a relief wall decoration – so that a particular objective is achieved. At other times the work may be broader, perhaps on a theme of people, or buildings, or containers, or exploring a material. In both contexts it is vital that there is room for the children to do their own thinking and to make practical contributions.

As part of the planned experiences, I have always included regular opportunities for children to choose their own media and themes. This is something to work towards over a period if the children need practice in making decisions. Choice can be extended from a simple one between two media, towards selecting any available medium which they have used before and a theme of their own choice. Some children may need more support and reassurance than others, but for all children I prefer to discuss the opportunity well in advance, defining the available resources, discussing ideas which they suggest individually, talking about ways in which to prepare and giving them a few days to consider their ideas and assemble information, ready for discussion with the teacher.

Launching a new project should be an exciting occasion where the children's ideas and imagination are let loose. Themes can come from any part of the curriculum; they can grow out of environmental issues, or school or local events. Most themes will be part of a planned curriculum, but there may be occasions when we can capitalise on a unique event or happening. The visit by an artist to the school, or a trip to a special exhibition, can lead to all kinds of projects, inspired by the themes, techniques or approaches seen, but drawing on the childrens' own interpretations and techniques.

I have found that some of the most successful three-dimensional work has involved thorough preparation by the children before launching into the main task. This is especially the case with older age groups. It may mean providing direct experiences of aspects of the theme under consideration, or access to reference material, which lead to talking, deducing, writing, and making sketch models. This preparation builds up a bank of information for the children before they select and test more personal and imaginative responses through further sketch models. It also gives a basis for making decisions about choosing suitable materials and processes to fulfil particular ideas.

There are times in the school year when it can be a wonderful boost to the sense of belonging for the children in a class, year group, or whole school to focus upon a common concern. This may be a festival, a celebration or a community activity requiring involvement or support from the school. If the transformation of part of the environment of the school, or the construction of a large scale structure outside is required, the teacher must obviously set the parameters, coordinate the work and delegate responsibilities. On the other hand, ways have to be found to ensure that the children take more than just a labouring role. Telling the class exactly what to do may be the easiest way, but it is not very effective educationally. Discussion with the children usually produces plenty of ideas. I have occasionally felt misgivings at some of the suggestions raised, but been surprised how, with a minimum of guidance (which is usually of a technical nature, or establishes a scale for communal work), children can work their ideas through and produce results which are fresh, lively, but most importantly, their own.

Other occasions call for the production of items to take home, perhaps to further the importance of the home-school relationship.

Here again it is important that children make the maximum contribution to the task, both by way of ideas and execution. Examples could include making a clay model as a gift for a parent, or a simple wooden toy for small brothers or sisters, to mark a festival day.

Amongst the children we teach there are always some who are unsure of their ability to produce work, especially when they have a disadvantage. Direct adult help may be required for cutting wire, producing a clay slab, cutting with a craft knife. In some cases I have acted as the hands, but only doing what the child has indicated, in order to fulfil his or her intentions.

The success of three-dimensonal work, by its nature, depends heavily on the provision and organisation of tools, materials and equipment, as we will discuss later. Initial distribution should ensure that the children have most things to hand where they are working, and they should have easy access to other items which may be required, to save movement and time. This is especially important to release the teacher for more critical aspects of teaching. Children of any age should take a full part in cleaning up the room and returning tools to the correct place after each lesson. It may seem quicker for an adult to hand out materials and equipment or to clean up a room than for thirty children to do it, but in the long term it is good education for children to make some decisions about what they require for their task and to clear up after themselves.

5 Getting started

Worthwhile three-dimensional work can start with a minimum of resources. A few bags of clay, scrap materials, adhesives and home-made tools and equipment are all that are required. At a later stage children should learn the importance of 'craft' and practice techniques and skills within the context of their work which may need additional, more specialised tools. Above all, children should be encouraged to use the most basic yet sensitive tools they possess, their own hands.

If a material or technique is new to the teacher, a few minutes spent experimenting with the material will remove any uncertainties. After time spent alone (or, better still, with colleagues), cutting, bending and joining wire, rolling and welding clay, or mixing and feeling the changes of state of setting plaster, the mysteries will disappear. Even more helpful could be a professional development session for the school staff.

My own priority is to ensure that children experience the range of thinking which they require, such as observing, analysing, using their imaginations, making decisions, discriminating and building knowledge. The children's own ideas, previous experiences and cultural roots are the essential foundation upon which to build.

Themes, topics or subject matter may come from anywhere in the curriculum, but equally the work may be based on the elements at the core of art and design.

EXPLORING TO LEARN

Children start exploring matter, forms, textures and space at a very early age. Touching, grasping and shaking anything and everything that is in reach are part of a baby's natural curiosity. Babies use their hands and mouth to find out about qualities of hardness or softness, taste and sound. Coordination of hand and eye, and their ability to judge distances comes through practice. With mobility comes a further need to find out about their environment. Crawling behind furniture, round corners, through doors reveals to them the spaces in which they live. They love to find enclosed spaces, in cupboards, boxes, under furniture, seemingly to claim their own territory or find a place of security.

Figure 23 Exploring sand (ages 3 and 5)

Their investigations extend to materials which respond to their actions. Porridge, water, sand, paper, fabrics, and piles of plastic beakers are ready targets for manipulation or demolition (see figure 23).

Many playgroups and nurseries provide for the continuation of these learning experiences through the provision of sand and water trays and the use of dough, plasticine and clay. These materials are responsive to fingers and minds, with great potential for promoting conversation and extending vocabulary, both between children and with adults (see figure 24). Working with large or small building blocks, either on the floor or on the table, allows children to define spaces and to construct (see figure 25). Cardboard boxes can be climbed into for imaginative or fantasy situations involving houses, cars, boats or space vehicles. For effective learning, opportunities to participate in these activities should be frequent, so that ideas, manipulative skills and self-confidence in their own ability to operate can be developed.

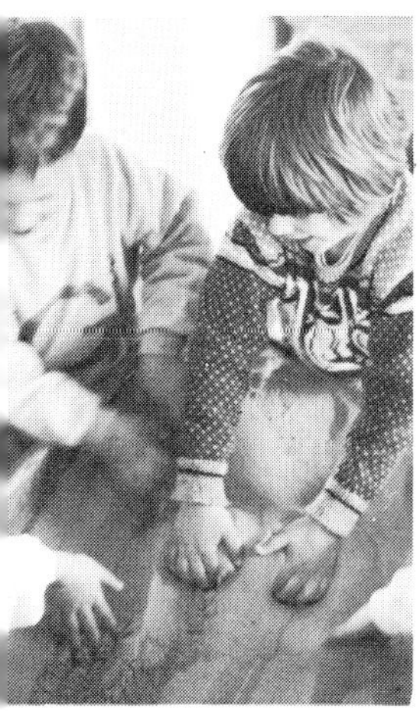

ure 24 Dry sand in a sand y (age 5)

When working with children who have special educational needs, I have found these sensory types of activity to be particularly effective. Handling materials and objects, and making things which are

Figure 25 Defining a space with wooden blocks (age 4)

tangible and therefore have their own reality, can give satisfaction and a feeling of achievement, especially to children for whom communication is very restricted and work on paper difficult. In extreme cases of sensory deprivation, I have used pieces of clay as a way of getting a purposeful response when other channels are limited.

Children who have had direct access to materials as part of their pre-school learning will be ready for a more structured approach to their tasks once at school, which may be self-motivated, or as a result of conversation with their teacher. Activities in the sand or water tray are at their most productive when there is discussion and purpose to the explorations. This can help to develop children's vocabulary as well as to extend their expectations of what can be done. Children who have had limited opportunities to experience materials will need to exercise their natural curiosity, making their own discoveries and gaining confidence, before facing more structured tasks.

It is very important to make basic materials available from an early stage, in order that children learn to manipulate responsive materials (for which purpose I find clay to be the best), and to construct and build using blocks, boxes and other rigid materials such as timber, metals and plastics. Through these activities children can apply their imagination to produce their own ideas, responses and fantasies. The overall purpose is for children to learn the skills of responding to materials, thinking, and designing. Coordination and the ability to use ideas to a purpose are steadily built up through a variety of activities.

Constructional kits or toys have a part to play in developing dexterity and inventiveness, especially when the instruction book is hidden! There is value in being able to follow diagrams and instructions, but children must be allowed to use their own ingenuity in their response to a constructional system. From this it follows that

Figure 26 Constructing (age 5)

kits which provide a good range of units, and which are not necessarily designed to make a specific model, give most scope for thinking, inventing and learning (see figure 26).

CLAYWORK: SLABS, TILES AND PINCH POTS

Following their own initial explorations, children can be given tasks, challenges or even games to play, to give more structure to their work. Initially a handful of clay can be pressed, squeezed, rolled and talked about (see figures 27a and b). Then it is 'how tall can you make a tower which will stand up?', 'how many holes can you make through your piece of clay?', or 'how many spikes can you squeeze from the ball of clay?' or 'how can you make the surface of the clay interesting to touch (with closed eyes)?'

Figure 27a Initial exploration of clay (age 5)

Figure 27b Manipulating clay (age 5)

Working in small groups, children can be asked to produce a form which is good to feel, and in contrast, one which is difficult or unpleasant to hold. Models can be passed to neighbours who describe how they feel, again with closed eyes.

Very occasionally a child may be reluctant to touch an earthy material, possibly stemming from fastidiousness or fear of dirtying their hands or clothes. I have found the use of simple tools to touch, then penetrate or texture a piece of clay usually leads to the tentative use of fingers, followed by a growth of confidence and then wholehearted involvement, all within a matter of minutes.

As these experiences with clay continue, knowledge of the material and skills begin to be useful in activities that go beyond exploring the material itself. They can be used to reconstruct observations and investigations in all parts of the curriculum (see figure C46 on page 127 of the colour section). Children quickly start to manipulate the clay into forms and shapes which become heads, figures, animals and buildings if they feel secure in handling it (see figures C47, C48, C49, C50 and C51 on pages 127, 128 and 129 of the colour section). Some children particularly enjoy producing fantasy creatures as there is no pressure to represent real things accurately. With practice children learn greater control and produce more complex symbols, both are steps towards the ability to work in a representational way. It must always be remembered that the discipline of the material itself precludes an exact replica and that the real aim is to interpret the character of the item looked at.

It is helpful to explain to children that their models will be more secure if they pull out (extrude) as many parts as they can from their lump of clay rather than join separated components together. Clay is sticky when damp, but as it dries, the surfaces can fail to stay together unless they are welded in some way.

Figure 28 Early representations of people (ages 4, 5 and 6)

When children have had considerable experience of manipulating clay into the forms they require, which may be on any theme such as figures, animals or abstract forms (see figure 28), possibilities can be extended considerably by a few techniques which are best taught in a direct way with a clear demonstration of what is involved. These are the production of slabs or tiles, rolling coils and ways of joining clay securely.

Joining clay

The traditional method for joining clay is to use a creamy mixture of clay and water (called slip), as an adhesive. Surfaces to be joined are roughened by scratching with a tool and then coated with slip before the pieces are pressed firmly together. In the classroom it is easiest to provide a small plastic container with prepared slip or a piece of clay which can be rubbed with a wet brush to produce slip.

In classrooms, especially with younger children, I find slip does not always stick and can create excessive mess. Most joining can be done by welding the clay. This involves mixing the clay from both sides of a joint with a modelling tool and then smoothing a worm of clay along the joint if necessary. Though easy to do, this needs discussion and demonstration so that it is done well, as models that split when dry or fired can be disappointing.

Slabs and tiles

Slabs of clay of even thickness may be used as tiles for an exercise in tessellation or as a surface to work on with colour or texture. If a slab is thick enough, the clay can be pinched into shapes, or hands, objects or tools can be impressed into the surface (see figure 29). Combs and sawblades make good scrapers, and tools can be used to cut into the clay. Although the slab is flat, it can be any shape, and the decoration upon it need not be tied down to rigid geometric patterns. Indeed, amorphous decorative shapes allow a freedom of handling, especially in the early stages, that cannot be achieved when children are trying to produce representational or constrained designs (see figures C52 and C53 on page 130 of the colour section).

Clay relief panels can be decorative, or tell a story, or show facades of buildings, perhaps as part of a group project producing a whole

Figure 29 A leaf rolled onto a clay slab and fired and glazed (age 7)

Figure 30 A row of houses made from clay slabs (age 8)

street (see figure 30). Faces and masks, or landscapes such as hills, valleys and islands can be made by placing the slab over a suitable form. An inverted dish, a pile of damp sand or some crumpled paper can provide this support.

Joining slabs by welding or with slip, gives us the means of making boxes, models of buildings, cylindrical or rectangular pots or abstract structures.

To make slabs, place a lump of clay on a piece of polythene or coarse cloth such as hessian, and roll it out like pastry, working from the middle of the mass to the edges with a rolling pin. Place rolling guides – strips of timber of the desired thickness – on either side of the clay to ensure that the slab's thickness is even when the roller runs freely along them.

An alternative method is to use a 'harp' slab cutter. To use the cutter, place a block of clay on a piece of polythene and draw the cutter towards yourself, so that an even slice is cut from the bottom of the block. This slab is removed and the process repeated. The cutting is helped by a child pressing the polythene firmly onto the table as the clay is cut (see figure 31). The surface produced when cutting coarse clays can be attractive in itself or it may be compacted by the gentle use of a rolling pin. The harp provides a quick way of supplying a group of children with slabs. Produced in this way, slabs are easier to handle if they are left attached to the piece of polythene, especially when using large slabs. With the polythene on the outside acting as a membrane, a slab of clay can be easily shaped, curved, twisted or made into a cylinder. When making a box or building, a piece of ply or hardboard can be used as a support to keep the slab flat until it is securely fixed in place (see figures C54, C55 and C56 on pages 131 and 132 of the colour section).

Figure 31 Cutting clay slabs with a harp

Pinch pots

Pinch, or thumb pots are a very simple way to make a variety of forms. They are best tackled when the children have had experience of handling clay, so that they understand how it behaves and have reasonable control of the material. The child pushes a thumb into a smooth ball of clay, about 5 cm in diameter, and by pinching evenly with fingers and thumb around the ball, produces a small bowl shape. Particular attention should be paid to the rim, and any little cracks should be carefully smoothed.

Forms made in this way can be used as surfaces on which to experiment with decoration, by burnishing with the back of a spoon, texturing, incising, adding clay, coloured slip or, when fired, glaze. Even more exciting are the possibilities of joining two or more pinch pots together to make a cluster or an enclosed form. These can be developed into models such as animals, figures, non-figurative forms or for experiments with oil lamps or ocarinas.

This approach can be taken further by pressing a fist into a large piece of clay and working around the form with both hands (see figure 32) to produce a thump, rather than a thumb pot!

Figure 32 A shell form made from a 'thump' pot, fired and glazed (age 10)

With these technical skills for claywork, children can tackle all manner of forms and structures.

DRAWING WITH WIRE

Wire can be used to draw a three-dimensional outline, or to provide a structural analysis, rather like a skeleton, or for exploring movement in people, animals, trees, plants, or the structure of furniture, buildings and so on (see figures 33a, b and c). The results can be lively and elegant and two- or three-dimensional.

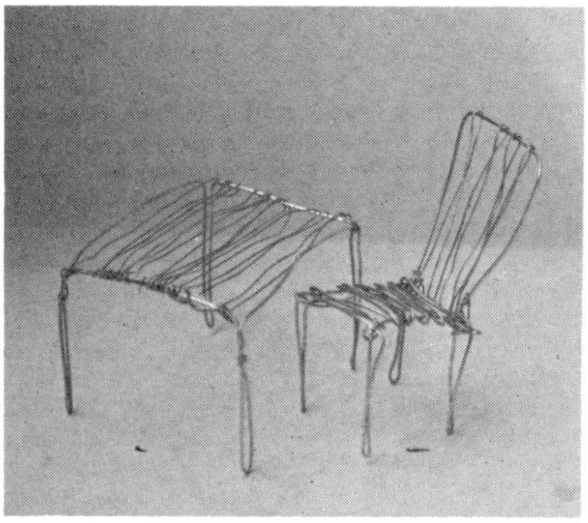

Figure 33a Wire drawing of furniture (age 10)

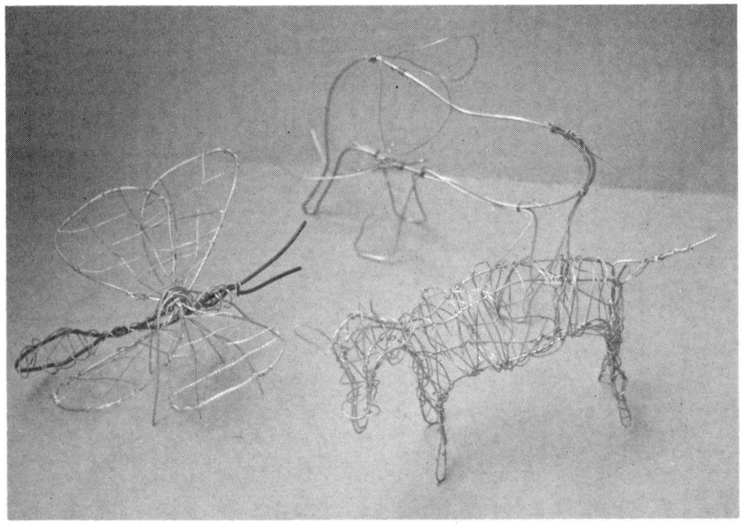

Figure 33b Wire drawing of creatures from imagination (age 10)

Figure 33c Wire trees from direct observation (age 9)

When working with wire children need to cut, bend and join. This means a brief demonstration by the teacher and a little practice by the children. Cutting is usually done with sidecutting pliers which cut by a simple squeeze; this deals with most thicknesses. For thicker wire it may be necessary to work around the wire, giving a series of nips, and then to bend the wire back and forth several times until it parts. Bending wire into shapes can be done with fingers or pliers, but a bench vice can help if the wire is very stiff.

Joining can be done by twisting wire together, using pliers to make it tight, but more often I use a thin wire to bind thicker wires together. Make two or three tight turns of thin wire around those to be joined and then twist the ends of the thin wire together with the pliers (see figures C57 and C58 on page 133 of the colour section).

PLASTER CASTING

Casting enables us to record a surface or form in a permanent way. It involves taking an impression in reverse, called a mould. A cast is a positive, produced from the mould, which reproduces the original form. By impressing objects or modelling in reverse on a clay surface, a mould can be created from which to produce a cast. Experiments with texture, pattern and shape can be fulfilled in a tangible, convincing way. Plaster will record the finest detail, for example, a cast taken from a mould made by carefully pressing leaves onto clay with a rolling pin will show every detail of the leaf's vein structure.

A simple introduction is for several children to make a clay tile each, on which they can build, cut away the surface and create texture, possibly using an agreed theme. Place the tiles side by side, face up, in a polythene-lined box or tray. Pour plaster over the tiles to a thickness of about 1.5 cm (which can be reinforced with scrim or wire), to produce a combined panel. Leave the plaster to set until it feels hard, which may be an hour or more, before turning over and peeling the clay carefully from the plaster. Individual casts of any size can be produced in a similar way by surrounding the tile or panel with a wall of clay, hardboard or timber to contain the liquid plaster. Larger panels may require stronger reinforcement with scrim and wire. Wire loops can be embedded in the back of the setting plaster to give a means of hanging panels for display.

Children can explore surfaces in the environment, such as tree bark, architectural friezes or mouldings, walls or weathered timber by casting. For this, children press a slab or lump of clay firmly onto the surface to form the mould, with hessian or scrim pressed into the back to hold it together. They then ease the whole piece of clay from the surface and placed it face up on a board. After building a wall around the mould, they carefully pour plaster over the surface to fill every part. A further thickness of plaster is added and suitable reinforcement embedded in the setting plaster. When thoroughly set, the clay can be removed (see figures 34a–34f).

Figures 34a–34f Casting from tree bark (age 8)

Figure 34a Pressing clay onto the bark

Figure 34b Reinforcing the clay mould with scrim

Figure 34c Building a wall round the clay mould

Figure 34d Pouring the plaster

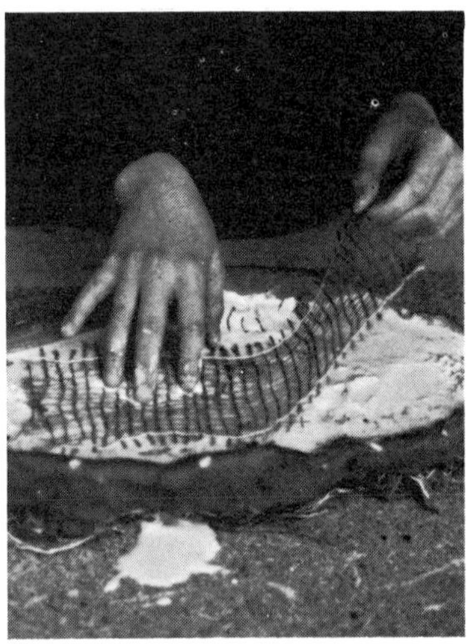

Figure 34e Reinforcing with scrim

Figure 34f The finished cast

PAPER AND CARD

Before children are able to use scissors they can tackle a range of tasks if they have a supply of pre-cut paper strips (see figure 35b), geometric or irregular shapes and some appropriate adhesive. Children can be given the task of making things that stand up from a surface. A card or paper base can provide a secure starting point. Loops or folded pieces of paper soon build up from the surface (see figure 35a), and the experiment can be played as a game to see how high it is possible to make the paper grow. Later, constructions with paper can be used as a means of developing cutting skills.

ure 35a Paper strips, folded and glued to a background (age 7)

Figure 35b Dragon made with paper on a fishing line stretched across the room (group of children aged 4 and 5)

Packaging of many kinds is readily available and can be used as a source for flat pieces of card, accepted whole as a container to represent an environment, or for box constructions. To begin with, constructions can be stacked without permanent joining, but later, PVA will deal with most glueing requirements. Cutting the edges of card to form tabs with which to join is a skill to be taught. In other situations separate paper or thin card tabs can provide a means of joining.

Older children who can use scissors can add more of their own ideas to the work, especially if they are shown how to score paper or card, that is to cut only the surface with the cutting edge point of the scissors (i.e. not right through) and then fold along the scored line.

This skill also allows them to add greater detail to models made from boxes and scrap materials (see figures C59 and C60 on page 134 of the colour section).

A surface of different levels and textures can be produced by glueing offcuts of paper, card and corrugated card, perhaps combined with coarse textiles (see figure C61 on page 134 of the colour section) or natural materials, onto a base to produce hills and valleys, a board for taking rubbings or an interesting surface for its own sake, enhanced by consideration of tone, colour and texture.

Children who have been taught to use craft knives safely can produce more complex shapes and structures. A good way to get them started in the use of a knife and to build up their accuracy is for them to cut through a sheet of thick paper on a cutting board in such a way that flaps of paper can be raised from the surface, with careful consideration of the pattern and variety of surface that can be achieved.

RELIEF PANELS

Panels may be made by sticking objects, natural materials, or images made by the children from material such as card or timber, onto a board or inside a box lid, using PVA medium. The resulting surface may be accepted as it is or varnished, sprayed or painted (see figure 36a). Kitchen or similar metallic foil can be laid over the PVA coated surface of a relief and pressed carefully around the shapes to give a more unified quality or added interest to the relief (see figure 36b and also figure C62 on page 134 of the colour section). Sometimes it helps to increase the depth of a relief by glueing small blocks of wood, card cubes or plastic pads behind flat cut out shapes.

CONSTRUCTIONAL TASKS

Simple constructional activity can begin in straightforward ways, using tightly rolled sheets of newspaper, held with a dab of glue or piece of adhesive tape. A thin dowel or cane, used as a core and then withdrawn, may help children to roll the paper tightly. These rolls can be used to build towers, dens, fantasy creatures, bridges, or abstract structures, using string or adhesive tape as a means of joining. Branches, garden canes, dowels or strips of wood, fastened with string

Figure 36a Objects glued to a panel and painted silver (age 10)

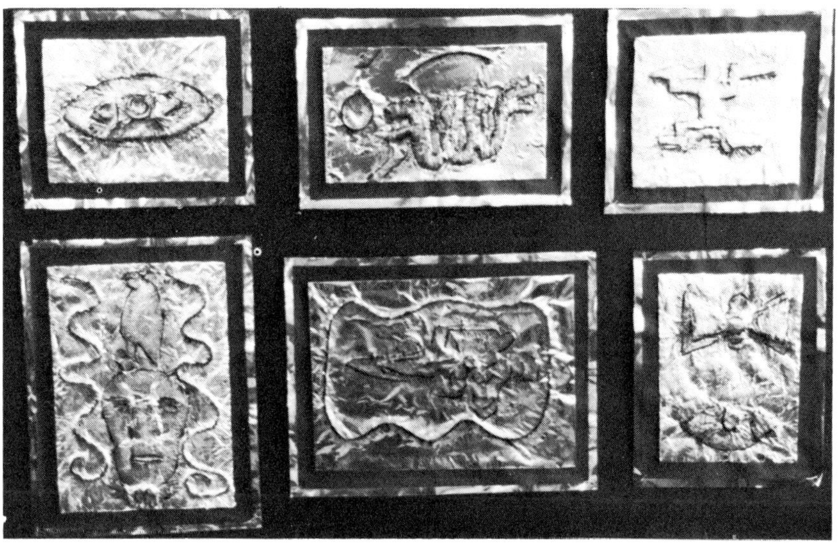

Figure 36b Card shapes covered with metallic foil (age 10)

or wire can be used similarly. It is possible to build very large structures by these means, even with newspaper, which can be very strong. Some constructional tasks may bring together a number of materials in order to represent different qualities of form and surface (see figures C63, C64 and C65 on page 135 of the colour section).

WORKING FROM ART, CRAFT AND DESIGN FORMS

All manner of adult work can be brought into school, from domestic items to abstract sculptures (see figure 37). Bringing a number of related, commonplace objects such as domestic pottery (teapots are an old favourite), containers made from different materials, old cameras or candleholders into the classroom, or finding objects which are unfamiliar, perhaps mechanical components from the garage, the working parts of a clock or natural items from the seashore, for example, can provoke discussion with children. Arousing curiosity or surprising the audience is always a good starting point for discussion and questioning. The activity can be used to extend vocabulary and powers of observation, deduction, appreciation and discrimination (see figure 38). It is rarely necessary for the teacher to have a full technical or historical knowledge about what is on show, but there are usually clues and pieces of information which can be researched, such as what things are made from, their function and place of origin. Drawing and model-making may stem from this experience.

Figure 37 Enjoying the feel of carved and polished timber

The opportunity to work with some items may be unrelated to the planned curriculum, and treated as a special event, but very often the objects will relate to a theme or topic being studied across subjects.

igure 38 An artist discussing is work (he is also their eadteacher)

Even more value can be obtained when the objects relate to the children's own practical work. The children can share a concern for the theme or subject matter which they find in the adult work, as well as the material or technique that has been used. Study of a relief frieze could lead to a group of children illustrating a story of their own, in a similar form, using clay. Seeing sheet steel sculptures could stimulate ideas for card constructions. A collection of ceramic boxes could result in children making their own containers, experimenting with alternative forms and surface treatments. The children should be guided into working out their own equivalent answers in practically every case, as copying is a waste of the children's thinking time and can prove to be a frustrating comparison for them. (See figures C66, C67, C68, C69, C70, C71, C72 and C73 on pages 136–138 of the colour section.)

6 Extending the activities

From the groundwork suggested in the previous chapter, many lines for development may grow, involving subject matter, use of source material, technical approaches and independent ways of working by the children. In considering these lines of development we have to bear in mind the range of abilities we teach and ensure that the interest, impetus and value of the work continues. This may mean consolidating previously known skills, using them as a vehicle for more complex themes, or presenting new technical challenges to the children which extend their mental and physical skills. On the other hand judgements have to be made by the teacher to ensure that each child has a reasonable chance of success.

CLAY WORK

Once children have learnt to manipulate clay, they can move on to modelling, paying greater attention to detail and making finer adjustments to the form (see figures C74, C75, C76 and C77 on pages 139–140 of the colour section). Clay can be removed by scraping and cutting or it can be added to the surface. Small pieces of clay firmly pushed and smoothed onto the surface should be secure for firing. This allows the children to explore more subtle characterisation when dealing with figurative and abstract work, to work in more detail, and to develop their feeling for form, shape and texture, as they create the variations of surface required on representations of landscapes or buildings (see figure 39).

A simple geometric form, such as a cylinder, cube or cuboid can be the start of many models. It may be a tube sawn from a carpet roll centre, ready-made packaging or constructed from clay. To these forms, children can apply ornament, exploring texture, adding shapes or colours, perhaps with thoughts of containers, or they can extend the structure by adding similar or contrasting forms, for purely aesthetic fulfilment. If made with clay the forms can be pierced or added to (see figure 40). A cylinder could be the core of a model, such as a tree, figure, or animal, a cuboid the base for a vehicle or fantasy machine. The children can use such forms as starting points for their own ideas.

Figure 39 Castle in clay, painted with oxides and glazed (age 9)

ure 40 Shell form in clay,
ed and glazed (age 10)

Making a well-crafted clay box involves measuring and cutting slabs accurately and joining them with care, which requires a little practice (see figure 41). Clay cylinders can be made quite easily by using a core, which could be any cylinder of slightly smaller diameter than is required, such as a rolling pin or the core from a roll of cloth. Wrap two or three layers of newspaper around this core before easing a slab of clay, with its polythene still attached on the outside, around it. After peeling off the polythene, weld the seam on the outside and

Figure 41 Clay slab boxes, fired, decorated and glazed (age 9)

then remove the core, which gives access to the seam on the inside for further welding. Forms made in this way have a pristine quality which suits some types of work, though on other occasions a more 'handled' appearance may be better.

Coils

These need practice but enable older primary children to produce more complex hollow models or pots. Roll a ball of clay on a wooden table or board, using the full length of the hands and spreading the fingers as they move over the clay. As the coil is formed the ends should be kept pointed, to avoid forming hollow tubes. For most work a coil should be no less than 1.5 cm thick and can be very much thicker if it is going to be used to make a large items; thin 'worms' are difficult to handle and join. Build up either as a continuous spiral or as separate layers and join them by thoroughly integrating the clay between coils, smoothing with fingers and thumbs so that almost a third of the thickness is moved across the joint. Normally this is done on the inside of the form first. The outside can be left showing the coils, 'nipped' with a modelling tool or fingers to form a decorative pattern, or smoothed as on the inside (see figure C78 on page 140 of the colour section).

FIRING WITH SAWDUST KILNS

This is a simple, direct technique for firing clay work, with distant historical origins. Most schools have a place away from the buildings, which can be used safely to build a sawdust kiln. This gives children close involvement in the firing as well as providing a satisfying, cheap and easy way of firing their own pots. I have known children to take over the whole process with the minimum of supervision, building the kiln themselves during the lunchbreak, firing overnight and emptying it the following lunchtime.

Build the chamber out of bricks or building blocks, about 35 cm square internally and 40 to 100 cm high (see figure 42a). Forty bricks will build a 40 cm high kiln. In still weather leave tiny gaps between the bricks, but place them tightly together in breezy weather.

Fill the inside of the hollow work to be fired, and the whole of the inside of the kiln with sawdust (figures 42b and c). Use dry sawdust

Figures 42a–d A sawdust kiln built by 5- and 6-year old children

from a local sawmill, DIY or pet store, mixed with a few shavings if the sawdust is very fine. For tall kilns, squares of chicken wire placed between the layers of bricks or blocks at suitable levels serve as shelves for the clay work and stop the work dropping to the bottom of the kiln when it fires. A metal sheet or metal dustbin lid can be used on top of the kiln (see figure 42d). Ignite the kiln from the top using crumpled newspaper. Once it is smouldering it should take between 12 and 24 hours to burn down to the base. Most clays fire to a dark colour, some are a rich black. Shoe polish can be used to produce a shiny surface if required, but the ware is not suitable for glazing.

RELIEF PANELS

Relief panels have a very long history as decorative features in architecture and as tellers of stories. Children can use them too, initially by exploring shapes and textures on clay slabs, impressing or scraping with any suitable tool or object, natural or made, and by modelling using hands or tools. These slabs may be fired or simply dried and varnished with PVA medium, to make them more durable.

Alternatively, panels can be made in plaster. Objects can be partially embedded in clay, covered in plaster and the clay removed, leaving the objects in the plaster, as a way of exploring relationships of form, shape and surface.

Another way to stretch the children's creativity and ability to visualise, is to produce modelled or cast relief panels using clay or clay with plaster. These can be produced by children working individually, or in groups where each child contributes a section. They model onto, or carve into, a slab of clay. Wire tools are particularly useful for carving, and can be made by lashing a loop of wire onto the end of a stick or dowel. Made as a positive image in clay, this can be fired in sections, or varnished when dry. Even more of a mental challenge is making a clay panel in reverse, as a negative image, and then casting it in plaster (see figure C79 on page 140 of the colour section). Some children need to work the implications through on a simple cast first so that they see the reversal of image and depths, but I have taught many who have grasped the idea of reversal quickly and have tackled a back, middle and foreground on their panel. The ability to visualise in this way is to do with confidence in using imagination or forming mental images. It invariably proves to be an exciting task for the child.

SAND CASTING

Casting in sand can produce bold shapes and images of any size. It can be used to make a relief panel or pierced or irregular shapes. It can be done on a beach or in the classroom, but it does require damp, sticky sand of the sort that builds good sandcastles. (On hot sunny days a small garden spray is useful for keeping the surface damp.) On the beach remove the dry sand over the area to be cast. Form shapes and broad textures by imprinting or scraping with hands, fingers, tools or items found on the beach. Suitable objects can be laid face down on the sand to be embedded in the plaster. Mix a suitable quantity of plaster and ladle it gently onto the surface of the sand. Reinforce the plaster with scrim or wire, and embed a length of wire to form a loop on the back for mounting or displaying if required. Leave until set before attempting to remove, which may take about an hour.

In the classroom a tray or container such as a shallow bowl or lid, lined with polythene and filled with damp sand can be used in the same way. When set, the sand can be washed or brushed off the surface of the plaster. A toothbrush is ideal for getting in the nooks and crannies.

WIRE AND ARMATURES

Wire can be used for its own linear qualities or developed into something more substantial with string, wool, fabrics, papier-mâché, tissue paper coated with PVA glue to give translucent, delicate surfaces, or with plaster (see figures 43a, b and c, and also figures C80, C81 and C82 on pages 141 and 142 of the colour section). Clay can be used for a short-term model, but because it shrinks as it dries and wire does not, the clay will crack. Wire used as a support in this way is called an armature. Wire netting, timber, twigs, string, and rolled newspaper are examples of materials which can be used as supports for work.

PLASTER MODELLING

Modelling with plaster is for more experienced children. It involves mixing small quantities at a time and working quickly, which can give the work directness and vitality. It is good for models of animals or figures in action, plants, trees and abstract structures. Usually a wire or wire mesh armature is used as a support, but twigs, timber, fabric,

Figure 43a Papier-mâché on wire armature, decorated with seeds and painted (age 8)

Figure 43b Figures in papier-mâché on wire armature (age 10)

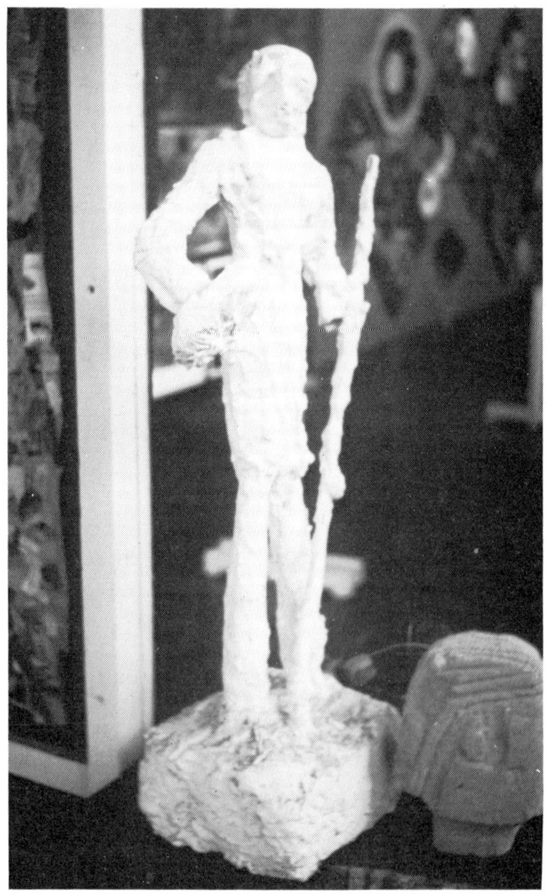

Figure 43c Plaster figure on wire armature (three children age 11)

string, paper tubes or boxes may be suitable. Surfaces can be produced using scrim, dipped in wet plaster, or Modroc dipped in water. These surfaces can be developed by applying plaster in a cream cheese state. As the plaster sets it can be carved, scraped, sawn or filed to refine the forms, though the quality of a simply modelled surface may be more appropriate and attractive than an overworked one (see figures C83, C84 and C85 on pages 142 and 143 of the colour section). Sand or sawdust mixed with the plaster, or dipping pieces of foam plastic into plaster, can extend the qualities to be explored.

BOXES

Children readily collect items which are precious or meaningful to themselves and find it satisfying to arrange them in a container (shoe boxes are ideal). Paint and collage on both the inside and outside of the box makes the container special and personal for the child. Alternatively boxes can be used on their side so that children can make an arrangement to be viewed at eye level (see figure C86 on page 143 of the colour section). These can be stacked to produce a class display and if lightweight items are used inside them, the boxes can be pinned to a display board. This may be extended to produce representations of environments, events or themes, using paper or card cut-outs, clay models or objects as appropriate. Older children may begin to develop their understanding of the concept of back, middle and foreground. Others may think of stage sets and work out drama situations in miniature. Coloured cellophane or tissue stretched across the top, with a viewing rectangle cut in the side, can be used to produce specific situations, such as under the sea, or particular dramatic moods.

CONSTRUCTIONAL TASKS

Blocks, branches, canes, lengths of timber and tubes can provide useful material for constructional tasks, using string, ropes or wire as the means of joining, so that modifications are easily carried out. For older children and more permanent work, nails may be more suitable. Hall floors, corridors, playgrounds or school fields are suitable spaces for work of this scale. Working in teams or groups can be particularly valuable. Children may begin by working on the ground, laying out roads, enclosures, patterns, or designs for a playground or garden. They can then pile or join lightweight materials together in order to build seats, stands, dens, towers, bridges, castles, fantasy buildings or creatures, rocking or abstract structures.

Thick plastic sheets provide a surface, or can become an island, pool or waterway if supported round the edges with bricks or damp sand.

I find that children can be endlessly inventive working with larger-scale materials in this way. It is a wonderful vehicle for language as children talk about their work, discuss and explain it and consider problems. It can also lead to dramatic activities in which the children enact events focused on a structure they have created, which could represent shelter, enclosure, platform, furniture, a means of transport or fantasy environment.

Each activity described in this chapter has variations and potential for further extension. Every encouragement should be given to the children to explore, experiment and develop their ability to use their own initiative. Creative work has no unbreakable rules or boundaries, but we can provide a core of experiences, such as those described, which gives a secure foundation from which to adventure.

The ways in which we extend the work depends to some extent on local sources, the resources within the school and the ways in which we use them. This involves planning and organisation which is our next consideration.

7 Organisation and planning

CLASSROOM ORGANISATION

Every classroom is different and every teacher finds their own best way of working, so it is inappropriate to describe an ideal situation. However, it is useful to share ideas about approaches to organisation and describe some of the facilities required for three-dimensional work.

A minority of schools have a special room for practical work, which can be helpful if it is available whenever it is needed: as we have seen, three-dimensional activity takes place in all parts of the curriculum and at any time. However, timetables may necessitate waiting for a slot, and this is usually too long to wait for primary children who need to continue with a task immediately. Even though a special room can be a great asset, facilities for three-dimensional work should be available in every classroom. Rooms with carpets may need floor protection in the form of a sheet of heavy duty polythene for plaster or clay work. Premises should be respected and cared for, but should not limit activities. The children's needs should come first.

Tables provide the most versatile working surface. Sturdy, timber-topped tables are useful for clay work, and an edge which allows for fixing a vice is an advantage. Most classrooms are furnished with laminated tables which are easy to clean for most activities, apart from clay which tends to stick very firmly. Boards of exterior plywood, hardboard or chipboard, with a thin coat of varnish, can be placed over table tops to provide a more sympathetic surface.

When using plaster, or other materials which could produce debris, I use furniture to form a barrier in a corner of a room, preferably the furthest from the door, to avoid feet spreading dropped fragments around the room. Making sure that all materials and equipment are available within that space avoids unnecessary movement. It is probably safer to use a bucket for water and another for waste, rather than operating directly with a sink, which will block easily. The children have to be clear that the barrier must not be crossed. When the weather permits, the alternative is to work outside if there is a suitable area.

WORKING IN GROUPS

A first experience of manipulating clay, where fingers are the only tools, can be arranged for a whole class. For most lessons though, the availability of tools makes it more practical to encourage children to work in groups, each involved in a different process. This also allows the children to select what they consider to be appropriate materials and it encourages a feeling of independence with a variety of outcomes. The success of most creative lessons is to be seen in the variety of work done. For new processes which require close guidance, rotating groups of six to ten children so that they can explore the unfamiliar activity in turn, gives the teacher the opportunity to monitor each individual in the exploratory group. Meanwhile the rest of the class can be involved with techniques with which they are familiar, so that they can focus on their ideas and interpretation of the theme.

Although the children are in groups, focusing on a material, process or theme, they may still be working as individuals. At other times it may be useful for them to work in closer collaboration. Tasks where each child contributes a unit towards a combined result, be it relief, a tile panel, a group of figures or buildings, have rich educational potential for cooperation and communication as well as the stimulation of working together on a creative task.

Taken to the next stage, the children design, organise and produce a piece of work together. This can be of great value but may call for mediation and careful monitoring by the teacher if the children are unused to working in this way.

STORAGE

Plastic trays can be very useful for storage when you are organising a range of different processes to be operating simultaneously: you can either place one containing the relevant tools in the middle of each table, or, assuming they are labelled and in cabinets or racks, allow children to get their own things as they need them. Large, stacking, plastic boxes are ideal for storing more bulky items, such as packaging and scrap materials.

Tools which are used regularly, such as scissors and knives, have to be checked at the end of lessons. Racks with slots for each item mean that it is possible to see instantly if any items are missing. More specialised tools like pliers or pad saws, may be checked quickly by using a shadow board, which has an outline of each tool behind the hook or ledge where each item is stored. This board could possibly hang on the inside of a cupboard door.

Solid work produced by the children requires standing space, when in progress and when completed. There may also be examples of adult work or reference items to be displayed. You therefore need shelving of various kinds, some to accommodate as much as possible in the smallest possible space, others designed for good display. In most classrooms this calls for some ingenuity! Some rooms have little spare floor area, others, particularly older primary schools, have walls which are almost completely taken up with doors, windows, cupboards and radiators. More recent classroom designs include extensive display surfaces for two-dimensional items but little for solid work. A solution I have used in a variety of situations is to make two 'ladders' out of timber, linked with shelves of blockboard, chipboard or thick plywood. The resulting shelf unit can stand on the floor, either against the wall, or at right angles to the wall to create work bays or to act as a room divider. It can stand on, or be suspended over, a bench. When placed in front of a window or standing on a windowsill, it can be particularly effective in highlighting the profile of objects and models. In every case shelves must be secured to a wall or the ceiling at the top so that they are stable and safe. Self-assembly shelving units, free-standing or for wall mounting, may be suitable for some sites. Another simple way to create extra shelving is to use bricks and planks – all you need to do is to put a plank of wood across two small piles of bricks, and you have a shelf. Add more bricks and another plank on top, and you have a small unit, which can be built up as high as you need, as long as it remains stable.

In some classrooms, high level shelves, just within reach of adults, can be a good site for labelled boxes and completed work no longer required for display but being kept for assessment.

Completed work or reference material should be placed somewhere where it can easily be seen and handled, so creating a special area at table height or lower is essential. A particular bench or table, rostrum, large box or board supported with bricks or blocks, should be kept purely for attractive display.

On a number of occasions I have seen teachers give responsibility for organising the room to the children, a real-life design challenge.

In some cases they have organised one or two parts of the room which they use for particular purposes, but in other cases children totally replanned the spaces, including moving the furniture, only directing adults for heavy items. Putting this into operation requires time for consideration, discussion and planning with scale models or shapes for trying out ideas. This leads to some noise and a great deal of debate during the big move, but the results are often fresh and functional. Inevitable adjustments have to be made by the children as they find problems, but the important thing is to accept the children's suggestions and to work with the room as they arrange it (which may take some time), even if the teacher's desk ends up in the store room!

COURSE PLANNING

Course planning must begin by assessing the children, their previous experiences, range of capabilities and developmental stage. Evidence for these will be built up from reports and records, but contact with the previous teacher and being aware of what happened before in the playgroup or classroom can give a better understanding of what the children have done. It is especially important to take account of the range of ways in which the children have been used to working, such as the opportunities they have had for independence, choosing their media or themes, collecting materials and equipment for themselves.

Planning may need to include activities especially designed to develop confidence and self-reliance. The social and cultural mix of a class can offer interesting potential for sharing ideas and attitudes. The overall aims of the school should underpin the planning process.

Every teacher has much to give to children but not all share the same interests and expertise. The needs of the children should stimulate the sharing of special knowledge amongst the staff, enabling them to carry out most of the three-dimensional processes. In terms of materials, fortunately most kinds of three-dimensional work can be tackled with a few simple tools, most of which are home made. More specialised tools and materials may be bought if there is forward planning. Other special resources may be available in the school or nearby. Access to museums and galleries, loan schemes, local artists or parents with special talents are all opportunities to be considered when planning.

NATIONAL CURRICULUM

National Curriculum requirements provide sound guidance about the main aims of each subject. Any meaningful art curriculum, as well as the statutory requirements, ensures that opportunities are provided for children to:

> undertake a balanced programme of art, craft and design activities which clearly build on previous work and take account of previous achievement;
> work individually, in groups, and as a class;
> make appropriate use of information technology;
> work in two and three dimensions and on a variety of scales;
> evaluate their own and others' work;
> understand and appreciate art in a variety of genres and styles from a variety of cultures, Western and non-Western.

The broad areas of 'investigating and making' and 'knowledge and understanding' provide us with a focus when planning a course.

Rather than using a materials and techniques basis for planning I prefer to begin with ensuring that the thinking skills are central, and soundly covered. Provided that the children have a reasonable range of malleable and rigid three-dimensional media available, omitting a particular material or technique is less important than would be the failure to provide opportunities to respond to materials, observe, visualise or make decisions.

PROGRESSION

The activities that we plan need to be appropriate for the year group, and to fit into an overall scheme of development covering all the child's years at school, and across the whole curriculum. Planning the development of technical skills is straightforward, provided the coordination, skills and ability of children to follow a sequence are taken into account (see figure 44). Some work, such as clay modelling and construction, is valuable for any age, but working with wire and plaster, for example, is more suitable for older children. The levels of thinking, ways of working and themes in the children's three-dimensional work should be seen as progressive experiences. Each type of thinking should be revisited in a planned way, with a greater challenge each time.

It may be that work which might be deemed a failure in regard to the end product could well have been a success educationally, as children learned from the process and were able to change and develop ideas for future work from the experience. This requires that the children have a degree of self-confidence and that there is sensitive teacher support for any apparent failure.

Figure 44 Bricks used to form a road (age 5)

Every part of the curriculum should have room for unplanned, unexpected activities. Some follow up a promising theme which has suddenly appeared from the planned work, others take advantage of unexpected events from within the school, visitors, local or national issues, or capitalise on the children's enthusiasms. Festivals or celebrations from any culture can provide wonderful opportunities for deepening understanding of social, cultural and spiritual matters, especially when the children are involved in practical ways.

DIFFERENTIATION

Three-dimensional work is mostly learned by doing it, and there are specific knowledge and skills which we can plan into the course. These give the children a base upon which to build their experiences and face the tasks and problems requiring initiative and trial and error. In looking at the levels the children achieve we must not lose sight of the nature of creative work, which means that it is often more important to measure our success as a teacher by looking at the variety of response than by looking for a uniform perfection.

There are many challenges in art and design which can be undertaken by children of varying ability, and which call for a depth of experience and response from each individual child. This, in fact, enables the teacher to provide rich stimuli for a whole group of children, secure in the knowledge that it is an appropriate multi-level challenge. For example a project on masks could produce a display of great richness in its variety. Much will depend on the quality of stimulation and emphasis when presenting the theme.

Children modelling reliefs in clay, or using clay as a reverse mould for plaster casting, can do anything from using simple shapes cut into or modelled onto the surface of a slab, to consideration of back, middle and foreground. The preparation of ideas and planning of the arrangement of forms usually presents the opportunity for the teacher to guide individuals to the most appropriate level for their work.

The teacher's knowledge of each child is essential to ensure that they are setting themselves appropriate targets which extend them. I have known many children with low expectations educationally who have suddenly been persuaded that they can be successful through the production of something tangible which they made entirely themselves. Attitudes and expectations can change dramatically in this way.

COURSE CONSTRUCTION

The core areas to be included when planning a course are:

imagination – visualising;
observing – analysis, selecting, recording and reconstructing;
expressing – responses, opinions, feelings, ideas;
fantasy – places and events created in the mind;
designing – making decisions, solving problems;
aesthetics – using the language of art;
discrimination and appreciation – in relation to own work and that of others;
understanding – the function of art and design in our lives;
knowledge – of art and design, past and present and from a variety of cultures.

This list can then be considered beside the materials, techniques and practical skills we use in three-dimensional work:

manipulating – clay, dough, plasticine;
modelling – clay, plaster, paper, card;
constructing – wire, timber, branches, canes, rolled newspaper, blocks, bricks, clay, paper, card;
carving – clay, plaster;
looking – at works of art and design.

These lists cover the basic needs of children and the National Curriculum requirements, though more facets could be added if desired. With them we can construct a simple table for course planning to include the main components children should experience. Taking one item from each column gives us a purpose and the means of fulfilment, which can ensure that the needs of the children are covered over a number of projects.

It is likely that as the work proceeds more than one item from each column will be involved, especially where there is choice for the children.

Thinking experience	**Skill**	**Material**
observing	manipulating	natural/found
imagining	modelling	clay
expressing	constructing	wire
fantasy	carving	plaster
designing	looking	paper and card
aesthetics		timber, metals, plastics
discriminating		bricks/blocks
understanding		works of art and design
knowledge		

Themes are likely to come within the broad categories of: **abstract or functional forms and structures, people, creatures, places and events.** (See lesson-planning sheet, figure 45.)

ASSESSMENT

Looking at children's work and evaluating the qualities within it, are essential if we are to make the children more aware of what they have done, to clarify expectations for future work and to decide what to do next in order to extend and develop their experiences. But teaching is equally concerned with matters which are not necessarily obvious in the finished work. Attitudes of enthusiasm and self-confidence, the willingness to experiment and explore, determination when things do not work out the first time, are qualities which I rate highly in any child and determine the nature of support and encouragement that I give. This indicates the importance of watching the children at work and recording these observations, while the points are fresh. Code words on a class list while the lesson is in progress, embellished after the lesson, is one way of building a picture of each child.

As teachers we should use the process of assessing as a way of questioning our own performance and planning our future actions.

In assessing the performance of children in their creative work, it is also important to have a view of their progress, strengths and weaknesses, none of which is necessarily evident from a single piece of work. Reviewing a body of work, together with sketch books,

<table>
<tr><td colspan="3">Class</td></tr>
<tr><td colspan="3">Theme</td></tr>
<tr><td>Thinking experience</td><td>Skill</td><td>Material</td></tr>
<tr><td>observing
imagining
expressing
fantasy
designing
aesthetics
discriminating
understanding
knowledge</td><td>manipulating
modelling
constructing
carving
looking</td><td>natural/found
clay
wire
plaster
paper and card
timber, metals, plastics
bricks, blocks
works of art, craft and design</td></tr>
<tr><td colspan="3">Areas of choice</td></tr>
<tr><td colspan="3">Cross-curricular links</td></tr>
<tr><td colspan="3">Stimulus</td></tr>
<tr><td colspan="3">Special resources</td></tr>
<tr><td colspan="3">Evaluation</td></tr>
</table>

Figure 45

Class 4 Year 1 (5–6 year olds)		
Theme Animals and their natural habitats Investigation and model making		
Thinking experience	**Skill**	**Material**
observing (circled) 2 imagining (circled) 1 expressing fantasy designing aesthetics discriminating understanding knowledge (circled) 3	manipulating modelling (circled) constructing (circled) carving looking	natural/found clay (circled) wire plaster paper and card (circled) timber, metals, plastics bricks, blocks works of art, craft and design papier mâché
Areas of choice Pairing Selecting animal Media – clay or boxes, card, scrap, papier mâché		
Cross-curricular links Drama Geography – habitats and climate Science – animal structure, movement, foods.		
Stimulus As a class – comparative enacting movements of animals Sharing and discussion of habitats from existing knowledge.		
Special resources Caretaker's dog to observe animal structure and movement. Video: 'Animals in Art' and sculptured animals from loan collection to be used at appropriate stages (midway)		
Evaluation Drama proved to be a good starting point, good comparisons and analysis of characteristics. Selection of animals, habitats and media took longer than expected. Considerable initiative shown in use of materials once underway, though most used clay for animals. Discussion of works of art lively and productive. (See lesson notes for details)		

preparatory items and notes of conversations for each child is a much surer way of proceeding. While we may remember most items produced by most children, we cannot always remember particular qualities, or see them in the context of a sequence of work and development. We may also require evidence to pass on to parents or colleagues. In the case of three-dimensional work, retaining evidence can be a problem where storage space is limited. Some work can be displayed and a sample packed away, but it may be necessary to resort to photographs of individual pieces or of groups in which each item is labelled with the child's name. These serve as a reminder of what was achieved, though no picture can show all the qualities of three-dimensional work.

Assessing creative work in any subject calls for subjective judgements. This may produce differences of opinion, but it is important that these do not diminish the value of creative work in the curriculum in the minds of those who deal in facts and figures. Indeed, I believe that the most valuable facets of children and their overall education are even more difficult to grade than is creative work. Marks have little meaning when considering attitudes to each other, to adults and a sense of responsibility, for example. Nevertheless, these qualities can be discussed and a picture of the individual can emerge quite clearly. Experience of public examinations in secondary school art and design has shown that teachers sharing the task of assessing and talking through the evidence can achieve a considerable measure of agreement.

At the centre of assessment is the need for children to become aware of their own strengths and of areas which require development. This requires planned methods and opportunities for self-assessment. Marks, again, mean little, but discussion with individuals can be very productive. It is an opportunity for children to learn to talk about art and design as well as their own products. Giving children genuine words of praise and encouragement as part of assessment can be a great boost to confidence and interest. Fitting suitable assessment sessions into the teaching day calls for ingenuity, but with young children the discussions are likely to be frequent and brief. Older children require a longer time to develop the conversation but it may occur less often.

Criteria for assessment

There are aspects of three-dimensional work which can be identified as being appropriate for assessment. These should be discussed by colleagues to select and define what could be included on a list which is manageable and understood. For example the list could be grouped under broad headings:

Technical appropriate use of materials and tools; making processes work; completing a sequence of operations; accuracy (see figure 46).

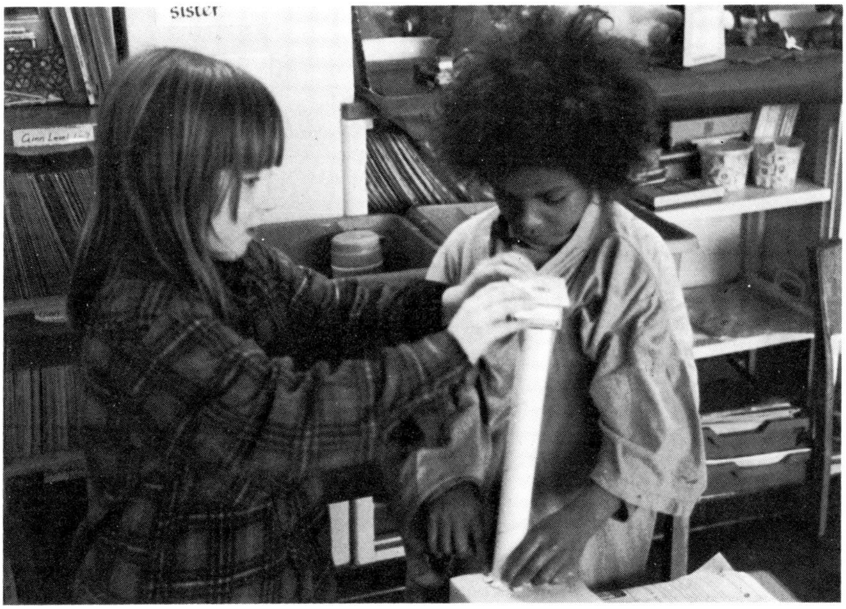

Figure 46 Fixing the giraffe's neck (age 6)

Knowledge range of vocabulary; practical knowledge of materials and processes; experience of the work of adults; different kinds of three-dimensional work, sculpture, architecture, designed items; different periods and cultures; applying knowledge to their own work.

Creative ability	do children have ideas, opinions and feelings of their own? Expressing these by products which involve making decisions about using suitable materials, forms, structures; work which shows variety of creative thinking.
Attitudes	Willingness to experiment with materials and processes, explore new ideas and use initiative; confidence in own ability to operate; reliability in application to work and clearing up; ability to concentrate and take work through to a satisfactory conclusion; patience.

Assessment should be recorded so that information can be conveyed to parents and colleagues in a simple, clear form giving the maximum information with as few words as possible. The parts of the assessment process which involve the children should have the greatest emphasis as it is through this relationship with the children that progress and development take place.

Bibliography

Adam, E. and Ward, C. *Art and the Built Environment*, Longman, Harlow, 1982.

Barnes, Rob, *Teaching Art to Young Children 4–9*, Allen and Unwin, London, 1987.

Best, David, *Feeling and Reason in the Arts*, Allen and Unwin, London, 1985.

Clement, R. and Tarr, E. *A Year in the Art of a Primary School*, National Society for Education in Art and Design, 1992.

Fulton, John, *Materials in Design and Technology*, The Design Council, 1992.

Gentle, Keith, *Children and Art Teaching*, Croom Helm, London, 1985.

Jackson, Margaret, *Display and Environment for Learning*, Hodder & Stoughton, London, 1993.

Josey, H. B. *An Eye on the Environment*, Bell and Hyman Ltd., and World Wildlife Fund, London, 1986.

Morgan, Margaret, *Art 4–11*, Simon and Schuster, London, 1992.

National Curriculum Council, *National Curriculum Documents 1984–1992.*

Reid, Louis Arnaud, *Ways of Understanding and Education*, Heinemann Educational Books, London, 1986.

Taylor, Rod, *Educating for Art*, Longman, Harlow, 1986.

Thistlewood, David (Ed.) *Critical Studies in Art and Design Education*, Longman/NSEAD, London, 1989.

Colour section – the qualities and practice of three-dimensional work

Figure C1 Exploring materials and ways of using them provides vital experiences for children

Three-dimensional work uses any or all of the elements defined in the text (pages 14 to 20). The following four pages show examples of those which are most commonly involved. One of our tasks is to develop in children a sense of excitement in observing, enjoying and using these elements

FORM Concave and convex surfaces, edges and corners, show the shape and mass of the object

Figure C2

Figure C3

Figure C4

Figure C5

Figure C6

Figure C7

SPACE Surfaces, boundaries and objects within can each help to define spaces and give the whole situation a sense of scale

Figure C8

Figure C9

Figure C10

Figure C13

Figure C12

Figure C11

TEXTURE Variety of tactile qualities gives interest to surfaces and often reveals the nature of the materials from which things are made

Figure C14

Figure C15

Figure C16

Figure C17

Figure C18

Figure C19

STRUCTURE Systems which ensure things stand up, interlink or maintain their form

Figure C20

Figure C21

Figure C22

Figure C23

Figure C24

Figure C25

Figure C26 Assemblage of geometric card structures from a whole class task. Age 11

Figure C27 Discovering the form which results from joining truncated cones (beakers). Age 10

gure C28 Developing a clay model llowing from drawing on location. Age 8

gure C29 Clay model, begun at the site and continued in the studio. Age 10

Figure C30 Papier mâché islands. Age 9

Figure C31 Models from drawings and notes made during a visit to a Mexican exhibition at the Museum of Mankind. Papier mâché on wire. Age 11

Figure C32 Mummy cases made with card and painted. Age 9

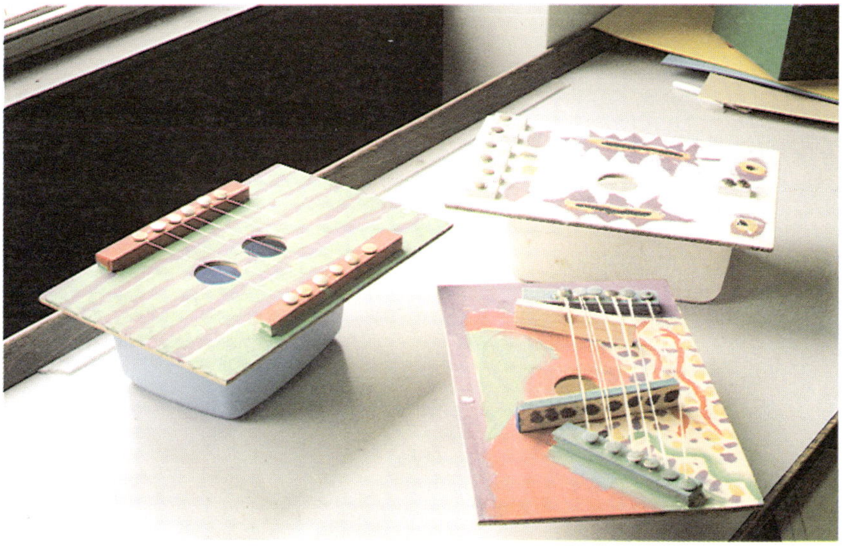

Figure C33 Stringed instruments made from scrap materials. Age 10

Figure C34 Using Lego to investigate the structure and design of a house. Age 6

Figure C35 Arrangement of natural materials. Age 8

Figure C36 Rearranging materials in woodland to form a designed area. Age 9. Working with older children

Figure C37 Forms made by twisting and weaving long plant stems. Age 10

Figure C38 Creature in an enclosure using twigs and materials found on the ground. Age 8. Working with older children

Figure C39 Early years exploration of a material. Dry sand. Age 4–5

Figure C40 Initial exploration of clay. Age 6

Figure C41 Lighting a sawdust kiln and witnessing the changes of state. Age 4–6

Figure C42 Exploring forms by the use of clay. Age 6

Figure C43 Developing the form of a creature. Age 6

Figure C44 Fired clay dragon. Age 7

Figure C45 Fired clay forms, enhanced with oxides and opaque white glaze. Age 7

Figure C46 Unfired clay islands exploring structure, form and texture. Age 7

Figure C47 Forest – clay model. Age 9

Figure C48 Guinea-pigs based on thumb pots, decorated with oxides and transparent glaze. Age 8

Figures C49 and C50 Large clay thumb (or pinch) pots based on the study of sea shore life, coloured with slips and transparent glaze. Age 10

Figure C49

Figure C50

Figure C51 Tree modelled from direct observation, developed from a basic clay cylinder. Age 10

Figure C52 Clay slabs, modelled in relief, decorated with coloured slips and transparent glaze. Age 11

Figure C53 Bird form, made with clay slabs, with coloured slips and transparent glaze. Age 11

Figure C54 Clay slab houses before firing. Age 8

Figure C55 Clay slab construction, developed by modelling. Age 7

Figure C56 A house and its surroundings developed from observation. Age 10

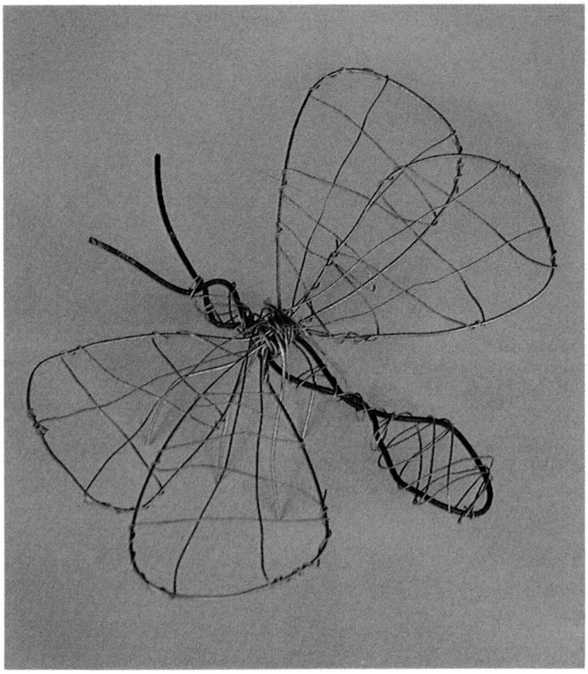

Figure C57 Winged insect drawn with wire. Age 10

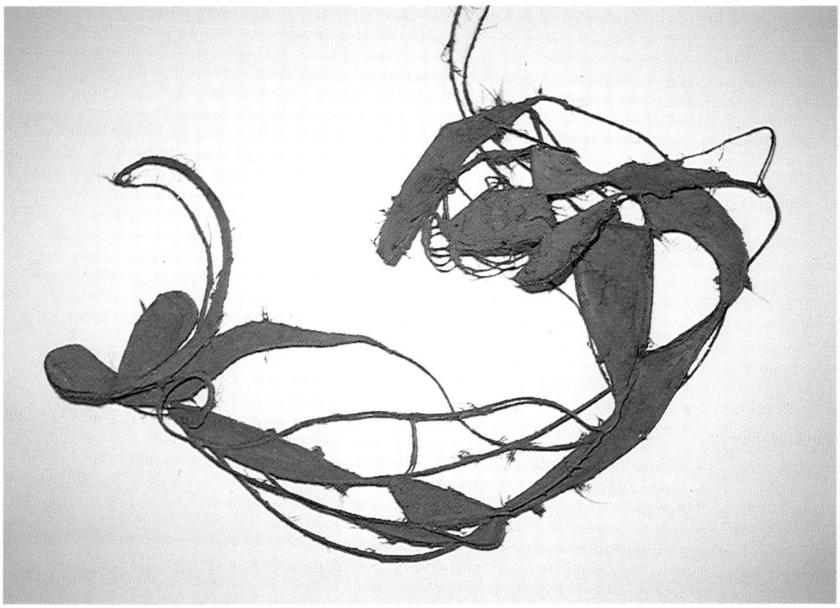

Figure C58 Wire dog with papier mâché additions. Age 11

Figure C59 Paper sculptured forms. Age 11

Figure C60 Painted card structure. Age 11

Figure C61 Exploration of a shell in relief using string to describe the surface. Age 10

Figure C62 Card relief panel with applied metallic foil on the surface. Age 10

Figure C63 Papier mâché island with trees. Age 9

Figure C64 Papier mâché tree trunks with paper foliage. Age 9

Figure C65 Boat constructed from a variety of scrap materials. Age 11

Experience of looking at and touching the work of sculptors and designers can stimulate considerable interest for the children and could result in them tackling similar themes. What materials and techniques, available to schools, could be used to explore themes such as these and produce appropriate forms, structures and surfaces?

Figure C66 Children examining carved pigs. They compared pictures, toy models and the sculptures. They preferred the sculptures. Age 6–7

Figure C67 Architectural relief

Figure C68 Cane structure seen at a Garden Festival

Figure C69 'Isomet'; David Hall. Welded sheet steel

'e C70 'Mauve inside'; Francis
and. Resin

Figure C71 'Hamlet in the Japanese manner'; Eduardo Paolozzi. Painted timber

Figure C72 'Oval form (Trezion)'; Barbara Hepworth. Bronze

Figure C73 'Two-piece reclining figure (no 4)'; Henry Moore. Bronze

Figure C74 Crocodile made from buff clay and glazed. Age 8

Figure C75 Fantasy creature, made with crank mixture by three children. Coloured with slips and oxides and covered with a transparent glaze. Age 10

Figure C76 Clay cats, finished with slips and glaze

Figure C77 Forms based on sea anenomes. Details picked out with slip and then glazed. Age 8

Figure C78 Heads developed from coiled forms. Age 9

Figure C79 Plaster cast made from a clay mould, modelled in reverse. Age 10

Figure C80 Figures in papier mâché on wire armatures. Age 11

Figure C81 Papier mâché on wire. Age 11

Figure C82 Tree and animal modelled in plaster on wire armature. Age 9

Figure C83 Plaster tree. The armature was made from direct observation. Age 9

Figure C84 Figure in wire and plaster. Age 9

Figure C85 Wire armature draped with strips of fabric dipped in plaster. Age 11

Figure C86 Room with figures and furniture. Shoe box, clay and card. Age 7

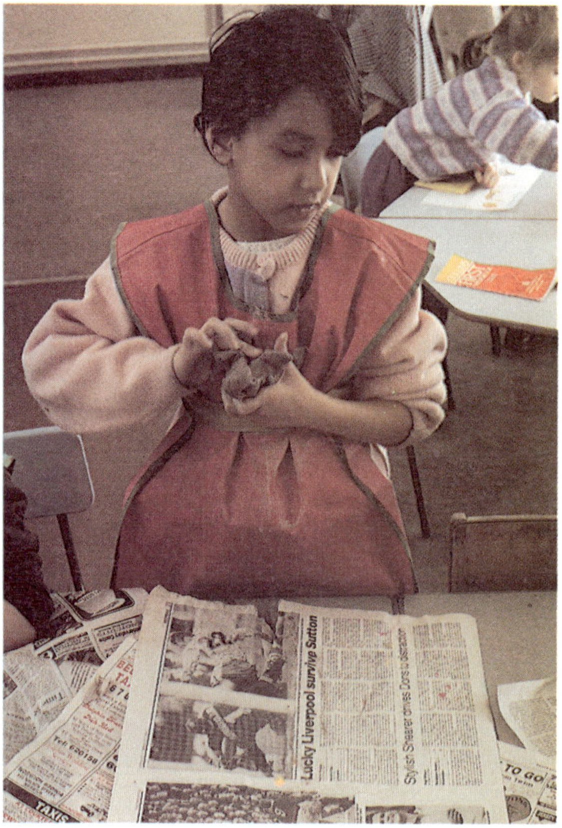

Figure C87

Figure C88

Exploring themes from any area of the curriculum, combined with experience of handling three-dimensional materials, can lead to the production of satisfying models and artefacts. This can inform children about many aspects of the world they inhabit. Just as important is the self-reliance and confidence which can grow from their sense of achievement